Praise for Rachel Waddilove

Rachel is a wonderful maternity nurse; a perfect addition to any household with a newborn baby because she is thoughtful, kind, calm, cheerful, organized, unobtrusive and very knowledgeable about babies. One of the things that sets her apart from other maternity nurses I've known is that she is a mother herself, and that makes a big difference. She also has such a gentle, understanding nature that she can deal with highly stressed and hormonal mothers quite brilliantly! She managed to get our baby into a routine of sleeping through the night very quickly, and that gave some semblance of sanity to everyone in the house!

Lady Ivar Mountbatten, June 2005

Rachel's flexible yet structured schedule was just the thing for our daughter. As we travel frequently, we cannot adhere to a schedule that is rigidly strict. Using Rachel's techniques, Apple was sleeping through the night at a six to seven hour stretch by six weeks. She was able to nap deeply in her cot and in her pram, which afforded me freedom. She was a very happy and settled baby right from the beginning. I believe this is because Rachel put us in a routine so that Apple always felt that there was a loving structure around her. She knew what was coming and could look forward to it with certainty. Rachel's advice on everything from breastfeeding to parenting was invaluable.

Gwyneth Paltrow, May 2005

D0188198

Copyright © 2006 Rachel Waddilove

The author asserts the moral right
to be identified as the author of this work

A Lion Book
an imprint of
Lion Hudson plc
Mayfield House, 256 Banbury Road,
Oxford OX2 7DH, England
www.lionhudson.com
ISBN 0 7459 5213 5
ISBN 978 0 7459 5213 0

First edition 2006
10 9 8 7 6 5 4 3 2 1

Acknowledgments

p. 79 Scripture quotations taken from the Holy Bible, New International
Version, copyright © 1973, 1978, 1984 International Bible Society.
Used by permission of Zondervan and Hodder & Stoughton Limited.
All rights reserved. The 'NIV' and 'New International Version' trademarks
are registered in the United States Patent and Trademark Office by
International Bible Society. Use of either trademark requires the permission
of International Bible Society. UK trademark number 1448790.

p. 180 'A Baby's Prayer' by Dorothea Warren Fox. Used by permission
of Charles Fox on behalf of the estate of Dorothea Warren Fox.

The text paper used in this book has been made from wood
independently certified as having come from sustainable forests

A catalogue record for this book is available
from the British Library

Typeset in 11/12 BerkeleyOldstyle
Printed and bound in Great Britain
by Cox & Wyman Ltd

The
Baby Book

How to Enjoy
Year One

Rachel Waddilove

LION

I dedicate this book to my darling children and grandchildren, who mean so much to me. I would not have been able to write it without them. To my son Ben, his wife Helen and their children Hannah and Jessica; my daughter Sarah, her husband Reuben and their children Zack and Bethany; and my daughter Jayne: thank you for all your encouragement to me to press on and write 'my book'. I do hope that you enjoy it and that you are able to pass it on to future generations in our family.

Acknowledgments

I am indebted to Dr John Tripp, Consultant Paediatrician at the Royal Devon and Exeter Hospitals, for his invaluable medical advice. Thank you, John, for the time you have spent reading and re-reading the script, for all your helpful comments and for writing the Foreword. My thanks also go to my dear friend, midwife Fiona Cochran, for reading the chapter on feeding and giving me helpful comments.

To my assistant Naomi Gilbert: I couldn't have done it without you. I'm grateful for your amazing computing skills, your superb ability with words and your unflappability. You have been great fun and lovely to work with. I shall miss the times we've had together in my study, and I'll always keep some Toblerone on my desk for you.

To all the families I've worked for: thank you for having me in your homes and allowing me the privilege of looking after your babies and children. You have given me much valuable experience and support in writing this book. Thank you for your wonderful quotes. It has been a real pleasure and delight to work with so many families, and many have become long-lasting friends. Thank you for all the feedback I've had which has helped to shape this book. It has always been the greatest joy to hear from parents I've worked with that their babies are contented, and are growing up into happy children. My gratitude also goes to all the parents I've advised on the telephone, whom I've never met, for encouraging me to write this book. To all those friends who are now grandparents, thank you for your contributions to my thoughts on this important role.

Thank you to Gwyneth Paltrow for wanting to be involved with this book and encouraging me to persevere. I am grateful to you for all your love and support. To Penny Mountbatten, thank you for all your enthusiasm and your endorsement of the book. A big thank you to Julia Cuddihy Van Nice for reading the chapter on routine, and giving me useful comments as a new mum. I am hugely grateful to Max and Sue Sinclair for their continual encouragement and for introducing me to Lion Hudson. To Rhoda Hardie and Morag Reeve from Lion: thank you, you've been very easy to work with and have always been there for me along the way.

Last but not least, my dear husband John: I couldn't have written this book without your support. Thank you, darling, for all your patience with me spending hours at my computer and forgetting we hadn't had a meal. Thank you too for keeping the house and garden up and running, and for all your practical help. You've encouraged me throughout to keep on going.

Contents

Foreword

This is a book for new mums and dads, which I feel confident will help to demystify the experience of parenthood and be a guide to parents with a new baby at home, through to the end of the first year of life. It is written by a hugely experienced trained nursery nurse who has worked in hospital and helped parents in their home environments over a number of years. Rachel also has good recall of her childhood experiences of being an older sister and of her own experiences as a mother. The author has clearly learned all the way through her life, and developed good tips and hints for minimizing the stresses and strains of parenthood. The references to her own experiences are limited but relevant.

Rachel helpfully lays out lists, routines and other useful information very clearly. I applaud the balance between routines (imposed by parents) and responsive parenting (for example, long-term demand feeding entirely responsive to a baby's crying). I agree that routines are invaluable but need to be flexible. Rigid routine is in danger of making us insensitive to babies' needs and at the same time unnecessarily limiting parents' decisions, whereas an absence of routine usually ends in a very stressful existence for parents, which may stretch into infinity.

The whole book is full of personal, understanding, warm and hugely useful expert advice, but is at the same time soundly based on a wealth of experience. Our babies need a warm and unconditionally loving environment to develop feelings of being valued, without which it is hugely difficult for them to meet life's challenges. Equally, however, they need a clear perspective as to who is in charge in their early life, to learn that they cannot always have their desires met – only their needs. Routines are the forerunners of rules, and dealing with the challenge of discovering that you do not own and run the world is critical to children growing up through the rest of childhood and adolescence to become socially aware and 'socialised' adults. It is never too early to begin the process of discipline, because discipline does not mean punishment; it is defined in the dictionary as 'the practice of training people to obey rules or a code of behaviour'. Thus, I used to give a lecture for midwives entitled 'Discipline for the Newborn'. No discipline means chaos, and chaos means stress. The key recommendations for structured but flexible routines coincide closely with the sort of advice that I give parents – and so must be right!

John Tripp

Paediatrician, father and grandfather
Consultant Paediatrician, Royal Devon and Exeter Hospitals NHS Trust
Senior Lecturer in Child Health, Peninsula Medical School, Universities of Exeter and Plymouth

CHAPTER 1

Introduction

Over the years in my work as a private maternity nurse with families, my clients have said to me on numerous occasions, 'You must put your methods of establishing a routine and looking after newborn babies down in print.' This has spurred me on to write this book. Before I go any further, let me describe my background and training.

My Background

I am the eldest of six children and my youngest sister is ten years my junior, so I grew up in a home where it seemed that there were always babies and young children around. I think that this is where my love of babies and young children began. My parents had a private maternity nurse for their first four children. I vividly remember this very official-looking lady in a starched uniform coming when my two brothers were born. I think my father was terrified of her, and I certainly was! I always remember not being able to go into my parents' bedroom to see my mother and the new baby, and feeling very left out. This experience has made me keenly aware of the importance of involving older brothers and sisters in family life when a new baby is born.

At the age of seventeen I attended a Doctor Barnado's residential nursery training college in Kent to train for my National Nursery Examining Board Diploma. My course at college involved working with many newborn babies, which I loved. I began my training in the 1960s, before the Abortion Act and before the Pill was widely used, and therefore a number of babies were brought into the unit to be placed for adoption. Part of my training was spent at St Thomas's Hospital in the maternity unit, which I also loved. I very much enjoyed teaching mothers how to bath, feed and care for their newborn babies, and that time in my life was a happy one.

Having completed my training, I went to London to take up my first job as a maternity nurse, looking after a premature baby. The baby was my responsibility for twenty-four hours a day, and I stayed until she was six months old. I then moved on to another family, with three children under the age of three, where I worked until my marriage. I married a farmer, and we had three children of our own. During those years of bringing up the children, I would help and advise friends with their newborns. Demand feeding was becoming popular at that time, and I could see that friends' babies weren't settled and they were struggling with sleeping and feeding problems. This confirmed my deep feeling that babies and young children need a loving routine and structure in their lives from an early age.

After moving to Devon, I returned to work as a nanny helping local mums with newborns and young children. Not long after this, I went back to maternity work, having been encouraged to specialize with newborns, as this was where I felt my gift was. I have travelled around the UK and the world with my work over the past decade. I now have four grandchildren, and have been able to go and help and give advice with them when they were born. This has been a real joy to me; there's nothing quite like working with your own family.

More recently I have set up a consultancy business in Devon. I offer daily home visits to couples who are expecting their first baby, to prepare them for coming home from hospital with a newborn. We talk through any fears and issues that they may have. I also do home visits to families with young babies, if they are finding it difficult to get them into a good sleeping and feeding pattern, to give help and advice in this area. As well, I give telephone advice to those who live further away and perhaps want some help and encouragement over the telephone.

The Aim of this Book

'Antenatal classes only take you up to day one and breastfeeding. It would be much more useful to learn about coping, washing, sleeping and weaning, rather than just breathing classes.'
Maymie White, fourth baby

My experience in working with families is that parents with new babies, particularly first-time parents, can be very fearful, as there are all sorts of conflicting ideas and advice given today. This is a primary reason why I wrote this book.

It is a very scary thing to come home from hospital with a newborn baby, whether you've had no experience of babies before or whether this is your third or fourth child. Often those first few days, and maybe weeks, after coming home from hospital can be very tearful times, particularly with the lack of sleep and perhaps the feeling of not quite knowing what to do. The early days after giving birth are different for everyone. Some women feel ecstatic and all set to get on, whereas others feel exhausted and wonder how they are going to cope with this little bundle of life who seems to want continual feeding, particularly at the times when they just want to sleep.

New parents will find that they are given lots of different advice by all sorts of people, with the best intentions. It is best not to listen to all you are told, but to decide on a particular pattern or plan to follow, otherwise you may get in a muddle with many different pieces of advice. Actually babies are much tougher than we're led to believe, and parents should not worry if they think they are not doing things the right way.

My aim in writing this book is to guide parents through the first year of their child's life. Many of my families have said to me over the years, 'It's time we had some good, sensible, down-to-earth, workable advice given to us to guide us in bringing up our families.' Society today has changed so much that we seldom have our parents and wider families around to encourage and help us with our newborn baby. My hope is that this book will be a comforting and helpful friend.

My Approach

I believe babies are a precious gift to be enjoyed as part of family life, and it seems sad to me that parents are often fearful of bringing any routine or structure into young babies' lives, as both babies and the family unit thrive on a good routine.

I'm a great believer in routine with flexibility, as over the years I have seen this work well in many families. This is how I was trained as a nursery nurse, and my own mother used routine feeding for all six of us. Routine is the beginning of healthy discipline. In my personal experience, establishing a routine in the early days of a baby's life makes for settled and secure children.

Breastfeeding

I'm a great advocate of breastfeeding, and have tried to encourage all the mothers I've worked for over the years to at least have a go at it. Most of my mothers have continued breastfeeding during the first year, and have always been pleased that they were encouraged to try. Sometimes mothers are not able to breastfeed, for whatever reason, and they must not be made to feel guilty. I have met mums who have had a lot of pressure put on them to continue to breastfeed when they were struggling and breastfeeding was just not working for them. If mothers want to bottle feed and not breastfeed, then I'm very happy to help with that, as in my view babies do well on the bottle.

Integrating Babies into Family Life

One of my main concerns is integrating babies into family life, particularly when they have brothers and sisters. It's important that your baby should fit into the family, and that family life shouldn't have to be turned upside down to accommodate the new baby. Many of the families I've worked with have found this perspective very helpful and liberating.

Sleeping through the Night

Getting babies to sleep through the night as early as possible is another high priority of mine. I have yet to come across parents who are happy to get up and feed their baby through the night for months on end. I know from experience that the more sleep people get, the more able they are to cope with life throughout the day. Some babies sleep through the night from an early age, and for some it takes longer, but it can be done. If your baby is still waking at night by the time he is six months old, it can be very hard to change this habit.

Teaching Babies to Settle Themselves

I find today that there's a lot of fear when a baby cries. Parents want to know when they should pick their baby up, and when they should leave her to settle herself. I believe in teaching babies to settle themselves as early as possible. This lays the foundation for a loving and secure routine.

CHAPTER 2

Needs for the Nursery

As you begin to shop for baby equipment, you will find that there is a vast and often overwhelming choice. The aim of this chapter is to help mothers-to-be decide what they need for their stay in hospital, and the first months of the baby's life. It provides shopping lists for nursery essentials, along with my recommendations and advice in the following areas:

- *what to take into hospital for you and your baby*
- *clothing*
- *somewhere to sleep*
- *feeding equipment*
- *nappies and changing equipment*
- *bathing and washing equipment*
- *travel equipment*
- *toys and playtime.*

Many of the items listed can be bought second-hand or borrowed from friends, and new parents will probably be given lots of gifts. In the UK, National Childbirth Trust (NCT) sales are excellent for buying good-quality second-hand baby equipment, and almost everything needed for a baby can be bought at Mothercare, Boots and John Lewis stores. Independent shops in the local area are also well worth a look, as they can often order goods in quickly. For any items purchased, receipts should be kept so that they can be taken back or exchanged.

What to Take into Hospital for You and Your Baby

It is a good idea to have your hospital bag ready about a month before your baby's due date, just in case. Some mums like to pack separate bags for labour, the ward, and their baby; however, this is entirely up to you.

Items for Labour

- antenatal notes
- birth plan if you have made one
- TENS machine if you are using one
- nightdress or large T-shirt for delivery
- thick socks
- snacks and drinks
- magazines and books
- dressing gown and slippers
- camera and film
- lip balm and facial spray
- wash bag and hairbrush/bands.

Items for the Ward

- two or three nightdresses or pyjamas – front-opening for feeding
- three nursing bras
- breast pads
- nipple cream
- disposable or cheap underpants
- at least twenty-four maternity pads
- two towels
- tissues
- make-up bag
- arnica tablets/cream
- anti-bacterial wipes
- phonecard or change for the phone
- clothes for going home (maternity wear).

Items for Your Baby

- newborn nappies
- three vests
- three sleepsuits
- muslin squares
- shawl or blanket
- clothes for going home
- warm jacket or all-in-one if cold weather.

Clothing

You don't need to buy very many newborn-size clothes for your baby, as you are likely to receive these as gifts. The ideal first clothes to buy are multi-packs of vests and sleepsuits, which are available in many stores and supermarkets. When shopping for clothes for your newborn, make sure they are washable, don't need ironing and are made from soft fabric such as cotton or terry towelling. You will find that your baby grows out of newborn clothes very quickly, so it's a good idea to buy most clothes in nought to three-month size. Larger babies may not fit into newborn-size clothes at all, and may need to start off in a nought to three-month size.

A newborn baby's circulation often takes a few days to stabilize, and I recommend putting a pair of bootees or socks on over a sleepsuit to help keep his feet warm. He will need a couple of warm hats to prevent heat loss from his head when out in the pram or pushchair. If your baby is due in cold weather, he will definitely need a warm jacket or all-in-one suit outdoors.

Newborn Essentials

- *at least six short-sleeved vests (bodysuits) with poppers between the legs*
- *at least six sleepsuits (babygrows)*
- *two or three cardigans*
- *one all-in-one or warm jacket for going outside in winter*
- *at least two hats*
- *at least two pairs of bootees or socks*
- *mittens (optional)*
- *bibs.*

Somewhere to Sleep

There is a huge variety of Moses baskets, cribs and cots available. Your choice will depend on the space that you have, and your budget. Small babies will usually be able to sleep in a Moses basket up to about three months of age. However, if your baby was 4.5 kg (10 lb) or more at birth, you may find she has outgrown her basket by six weeks. Once your baby is around 5.5 kg (12 lb), she will probably be more comfortable in a cot. I would usually recommend that you get a drop-side cot, as this makes lifting your baby in and out much easier. Make sure, particularly if you are buying second-hand, that the cot is sturdy and will safely hold your baby once she can stand up. You will also need to check that any catches or drop-side mechanisms are working properly. If you do buy a second-hand cot, I would advise that you buy a new mattress so that you can be confident that it is clean and safe. You can also buy cots that convert into a small bed when your child is older, but remember that you may need the cot for your next baby.

I usually find that blankets are the most practical bedding for newborns, as you can swaddle and tuck your baby under them. I would not recommend using baby sleeping bags (often known as 'grobags') until your baby is about three months old, and doesn't need swaddling. Duvets and quilts are not suitable for babies under one year, as they can overheat.

My personal feeling is that baby monitors are not essential, as they can cause parents to be anxious about every noise that a baby makes while sleeping. However, if your bedroom is some distance from your baby's room you may find a monitor practical.

Shopping List for Sleeping

- Moses basket/crib and mattress
- drop-side cot and mattress
- bedding for the Moses basket: at least
    four fitted sheets
    four cellular cotton blankets
    four flat sheets (optional)
- bedding for the drop-side cot:
    four fitted sheets
    four flat sheets
    four large blankets
- twelve to twenty-four muslin squares (place under baby's head to catch any milk he brings up)
- two shawls for swaddling
- room temperature gauge (optional)
- baby monitor (optional).

Feeding Equipment

The feeding equipment you need will vary slightly, depending on whether you choose to breastfeed or bottle feed. If you are breastfeeding and want to give your baby expressed breast milk from time to time, you will still need some bottles. You may be able to borrow or buy some feeding equipment second-hand, such as bottles, bottle warmers, breast pumps and sterilizers. However, it is most important that you do buy new teats.

There are a number of soothing nipple creams available, and I often recommend brands with calendula and Kamillosan (chamomile). I would highly recommend the breast pumps made by Medela and Ameda, which are widely available in the UK. The Medela pump is an electric pump which is small, portable and easy to use. The Ameda pump is also electric, and you can express from both breasts at once. Avent make a good manual breast pump if you prefer this method. If you don't want to buy one, you can hire breast pumps from the NCT (in the UK) and some local hospitals.

There are many different types of bottles to choose from, and it can seem confusing when you first start looking. I often recommend Avent as a good all-round bottle, as it has a wide neck which is easy to fill. NUK bottles are also very good, but usually have a narrower neck. Most bottles come with silicone teats; however, you can buy a softer latex teat if you prefer. You can also buy latex teats that are nipple-shaped, and these are good if you are combining breast and bottle feeding (such as giving expressed milk). You should use teats with a size 1 hole for around the first six weeks of your baby's life, unless your baby is feeding very slowly, in which case you may need the size 2 teat.

To sterilize bottles, you can use an electric or microwave sterilizer, or Milton tablets or liquid. I usually recommend an electric sterilizer rather than a microwave one, as you can take it with you anywhere. Avent make a very good electric sterilizer, which fits their bottles perfectly.

SMA Gold, Aptimel First and Cow & Gate are all good UK brands of formula for newborn or young babies. If you have a very hungry baby, you can move on to SMA White. There are also a number of organic brands on the market, including Hipp and Boots own-brand. When you're away from home, a milk powder dispenser can be very useful, as you don't have to carry around a large tin of formula.

Breastfeeding Shopping List

- *plenty of breast pads*
- *at least two nursing bras*
- *nipple cream*
- *breast pump, hand or electric*
- *freezer bags for freezing breast milk*
- *2 x 100 ml (4 fl oz) bottles*
- *size 1 newborn teats*
- *bottle sterilizer*
- *small tin of formula (optional)*
- *nursing chair (optional)*
- *nursing pillow (not essential; ordinary pillows are just as good).*

Bottle Feeding Shopping List

- *2 x 100 ml (4 fl oz) bottles with teats*
- *6 x 200 ml (8 fl oz) bottles with teats*
- *size 1 newborn teats*
- *bottle sterilizer*
- *plastic jug for warming bottles*
- *tin of formula suitable for newborns*
- *bottle brush*
- *electric bottle warmer (optional)*
- *milk powder dispenser (optional).*

Nappies and Changing Equipment

I usually advise that you don't buy too many newborn-size nappies, in case your baby is too big for this size when he is born. You can choose from disposable or washable nappies, and many parents use a combination of both. It is often a good idea not to buy huge quantities of nappies before your baby is born, as you will need some time to find out what works best for you and your baby. Square terry towelling or shaped washable nappies can be bought in high-street shops nowadays. In the UK there is also a very good nappy service called Cotton Bottoms, which provides you with nappies, collects them for washing, and delivers clean ones to your door (see Further Resources).

Barrier creams such as zinc and castor oil and Vaseline are good for preventing nappy rash. Sudocrem, Drapolene and Metanium cream are excellent for soothing and healing your baby's skin if it begins to get sore. Some people find it helpful to have two changing mats so that they can keep one upstairs and one downstairs. To protect your back, it is a good idea to be able to change your baby in a position where you don't have to bend over. You can buy a changing unit with drawers or storage underneath, or use the top of a chest of drawers, making sure that your baby is secure and cannot fall off.

Changing Shopping List

- *changing mat*
- *changing unit with safety strap (optional)*
- *cotton wool*
- *newborn nappies (disposable or washable)*
- *barrier cream for baby's bottom*
- *baby wipes (use from two weeks onwards)*
- *nappy bin or nappy wrapper (optional)*
- *disposable changing mat liners (optional).*

Shopping List for Washables

- *fifteen to twenty-five washable nappies*
- *four or five wraps or plastic pants*
- *nappy liners (washable or disposable)*
- *nappy pins or 'nappy nippas'*
- *plastic bucket with lid for storing dirty nappies*
- *nappy sterilizing liquid (Napisan).*

Bathing and Washing Equipment

There are a number of different plastic baths that you can buy for your baby; however, you can use a hand basin (being careful of the hot taps), a plastic bowl, or a regular bath. If you are bathing your baby in a large bath, you can buy a range of bath supports, which will last her up to about six months.

Toiletries for your baby should be gentle and suitable for sensitive skin; Johnson's is an excellent brand. There are also lots of organic products available nowadays. Liquid baby washes are very good for the bath, in preference to bubble bath, which does not rinse off as well. You can use baby oil or olive oil in the bath or directly on the skin, and it is also very good for helping to remove cradle cap.

Bathing Shopping List

- *two bath towels or baby towels with hoods*
- *two hand towels*
- *two sponges (optional)*
- *two soft flannels*
- *baby soap or liquid wash*
- *baby powder*
- *cotton wool*
- *moisturizing cream or lotion*
- *baby oil (olive oil is just as good)*
- *shampoo*
- *a soft hairbrush*
- *baby nail scissors with rounded tips*
- *bath thermometer (optional)*
- *waterproof bathing apron (optional but very useful)*
- *baby bath and stand (optional).*

Travel Equipment

The one essential piece of travel equipment you will need is a rear-facing car seat to take your baby home from hospital. It's important that you ensure that the seat fits your car, and that you and your partner know how to take it in and out of the car before you bring your baby home.

There are many prams, pushchairs and travel systems suitable from birth. Your choice will depend on your personal taste, budget and space available. I usually advise that it is worth buying or borrowing a pram if you have room for one, as your baby can lie flat, and a pram often has plenty of space for shopping underneath. Travel systems comprising car seats and carrycots that clip on to a pushchair frame can be very useful, especially if you are doing a lot of travelling. When buying a pram or pushchair, make sure that you are comfortable pushing it along and that the handles are at the right height for you. Check that it is easy to fold up and unfold, and that it fits easily in the boot of your car.

You will need a bag to carry changing equipment for your baby. You can use an ordinary bag that you already have, or you can buy a specialist changing bag. Most changing bags come with an integral changing mat and have space for a bottle. You can choose a rucksack or shoulder-bag style, depending on your personal preference.

Slings are a good option if you are going to be doing a lot of walking or using public transport, and you don't want to take a pushchair. Make sure you buy a good brand which provides support for your back. Your baby can go in a backpack-style carrier from around five months onwards. A travelcot is a good idea if you are going to be taking your baby away from home a lot. You don't need to buy this before your baby is born, as you can use a Moses basket or carrycot for the first few months.

Travel Shopping List

- *rear-facing car seat suitable from birth*
- *pram and/or pushchair/travel system suitable from birth*
- *changing bag*
- *baby sling or carrier (optional)*
- *travelcot (optional).*

Toys and Playtime

You don't need to buy any play equipment before your baby is born. In fact, you will probably find that you receive lots of toys and activities as gifts for your baby. Young babies seem to like toys with strong contrasting colours such as black and white. Often the first toys your baby will notice are black and white, and a panda makes a good first soft toy. When buying toys for your baby, check that they are suitable for his age and (in Europe) have the CE safety mark.

Babies don't need to have a chair to sit in until they are about one month old. Adjustable chairs, which recline almost flat, are the most comfortable for young babies. I prefer these to bouncy chairs, as they are more stable and will last for longer. Activity gyms and activity arches are great from around one month, and as your baby gets older she will really enjoy reaching out for the toys hanging down.

Playtime Shopping List

- *black and white baby books/toys*
- *soft toys suitable from birth*
- *adjustable or bouncy chair*
- *activity gym*
- *activity arch for car seat/bouncy chair*
- *musical toys/mobile.*

Final Thoughts

It's very easy to get swept along feeling that you have to buy lots of expensive equipment for your baby before he is born. As long as he has something to wear, clean nappies, somewhere to sleep and plenty to eat he will be perfectly happy for the first few days. You will find that there's great enjoyment in shopping for him once he is born, as you will have a better idea of what you need for him.

CHAPTER 3

Coming Home from Hospital

'Having a baby is like throwing a hand grenade into family life.'
Sophie Burrell-Thompson, first baby

Over the years many parents have told me that they were well-prepared for pregnancy and birth, but not for how they would actually feel when they got home. Often, professionals assume that parents will find it difficult to take in lots of information about coping with life after the birth. However, in my experience parents wish they had been better informed and had time to prepare for the emotional ups and downs of life with a new baby.

If you have had a hospital delivery, it is a good idea to stay in for a few days if you can, particularly so that the midwives can help you with feeding and caring for your baby. If you are breastfeeding, it can be very helpful to get support at this stage with latching on and positioning your baby for feeding. The length of your stay will probably be dependent on where you live and how busy the hospital is. If you have had a straightforward delivery and all is well with you and your baby, you may find that you are sent home fairly quickly.

This chapter aims to give an insight into the feelings you may experience when you first come home with your baby, and prepare you for the practical and emotional aspects of life with a newborn baby. I have been asked by lots of parents to write this chapter, so I hope it will be of help.

Registering the Birth

There are lots of things to think about after having your baby, and it is very easy to forget the paperwork. In the UK, you will need to register your baby's birth within six weeks, either at the hospital or your local register office. The registrar will help you to fill in the necessary forms and you will receive a copy of your baby's birth certificate. Either parent can register the birth, and you do not need to take your baby with you. Once you have your baby's birth certificate, UK residents are entitled to child benefit, and may also be eligible for child tax credits. You can find out about claiming these benefits from your local social security centre or Citizens Advice Bureau (see Further Resources).

Your Feelings

There is no place quite like home, and you and your partner will probably feel quite euphoric about bringing your newborn home for the first time. However, the reality of coming home can be very different from your expectations. You may feel wonderful as you gaze at your newborn in your own home, but at other times you may feel completely overwhelmed, especially if you are very tired and your baby suddenly seems to be airing her lungs more than she did in hospital.

Worries about Being a Parent

'My biggest fear with number one baby was failure... Most of us are used to being in control and have a secret longing to carry that control through to motherhood. It's a shock.'
Maymie White, fourth baby

We don't have the luxury of a practice run at parenting, and both you and your partner may worry that you are not going to be a good mum or dad. It is important to try to feel happy with yourself, as there really is no such thing as the perfect parent.

When you come home, it can be very frightening to have sole responsibility for looking after your precious newborn for the first time. You may feel inadequate and have a fear of not being able to cope, particularly when your partner goes back to work. Try to be as relaxed with your baby as possible, giving him lots of cuddles and unconditional love. Remember, too, that it will take time to get to know him, and by the time he is six weeks old you will be much more confident with him.

You may find you are given conflicting advice about how to care for your baby: fashions in childcare do come and go. It's a good idea to decide what your own approach will be, and give yourself permission to stick with it. Try not to compare your parenting with your friends, as you know your baby best and your instincts and common sense are the best guide to what she needs.

Mood Swings

You may find that one day you feel ecstatic about everything, and yet the next day you are miserable. These mood swings are quite normal, especially if you are breastfeeding. Some women are very weepy when their milk comes in at three to four days after the birth, whereas others feel weepy later on. I remember when our first baby was six weeks old, I cried and cried. My poor husband didn't know what to do with me, and I had no idea why I was crying.

If you do find that you have mood swings, try not to worry and don't put yourself under pressure to 'put on a brave face'. It's often best to have a really good cry and talk about your feelings with your partner or a close friend. As much as you can, try to accept that mood swings and tears are a normal part of life as you adjust to the tiredness and hormonal changes after birth. Even if your friends with babies appear to be coping amazingly well, the reality is that they will probably have had lots of ups and downs too.

Coping with Postnatal Depression

Many mothers I've worked with are worried about having postnatal depression, particularly if they experience mood swings and 'baby blues' in the first few weeks. The majority of women recover quickly from baby blues, but if you feel miserable and low for a longer period, you may need to talk this through with your health visitor or GP. Some of the signs of postnatal depression are feelings of being unable to cope, and a sense of everything seeming very bleak and hopeless. You may also feel very anxious and tense, or be unusually irritable. Physically, you may want to sleep during the day and yet be unable to sleep at night, and you may lose your appetite.

If you do suffer from postnatal depression, remember that you're not alone and that it is not your fault – most importantly, don't feel guilty! The best thing you can do for you and your baby is to seek help.

Talking things through with your partner, a close relative or friend can help, as can getting out of the house and doing some normal, everyday things. It's important to talk to your GP, who may prescribe anti-depressants. There are anti-depressants which are suitable if you are breastfeeding. Your GP can also put you in touch with a counsellor, or you can contact the Association for Postnatal Illness (see Further Resources). It can take time to feel back to normal, but do persevere, as the majority of women make a full recovery.

A Father's Perspective on Depression

Some fathers also suffer from depression after the birth of their child, as one friend eloquently describes:

'I can remember having some deep anxieties about being a father and anticipating a huge change in the way life was going to be. These thoughts became a cycle which I carried around with me during the last few months and weeks of my wife's pregnancy. I should have sought help before it was too late, but how do you open up to anyone that you feel and think such fearful things about being a parent? When my son and wife came home from hospital, I had to face the reality of being a daddy and that my life now was going to be changed forever! I also had to face the reality that I could not deal with it and as a consequence it all became like a tidal wave, washing over me and I was trying desperately not to let go. The thing that really hurt and confused me was that this was supposed to be the happiest time in my life, and all I could do was focus on the deep-seated fears and confusion.

'Whatever medical label best suited my condition, I did get help. Through the help of my patient and non-judgmental wife, the love of close friends and family, a good GP, and a gifted counsellor I started on the long road to recovery. I now believe the day I started the journey towards wholeness was the day my son came home from hospital. I was off work a long time, which actually meant I got to spend time with him and this meant I really connected with him and all my fears and worries were being challenged. My son has become a wonderful source of joy and healing and for this I am so grateful, as at one point over two years ago I would have struggled to believe it!'

Memory Loss

You may find that you are very forgetful in the first few weeks when you bring your baby home, for example forgetting when you last fed your baby or losing the end of sentences. Memory loss is often due to hormonal changes in your body and sleep deprivation. Your memory will come back, but give yourself a bit of time, as your body has been going through huge changes over the last nine months. If you are struggling with forgetfulness, have a notebook or diary handy and use it to jot down feed times and other things that you need to remember.

Tiredness

There will be days when you feel really exhausted, especially as you will be having broken nights. When you are very tired, you will probably find that you are more weepy and may feel that you are not coping with life in general. It can be difficult to make decisions and carry out day-to-day chores around the house. At this stage, the best thing you can do for yourself and the baby is to rest whenever you have the opportunity. Don't worry if you need to go back to bed during the day or sleep when your baby is sleeping. If you can, hang on to the fact that the extreme tiredness will pass as your baby gets bigger and sleeps for longer at night.

Your Relationship with Your Partner

The birth of your baby is a deeply emotional experience that you will share as parents for the rest of your lives. Most couples find that bringing a new baby home is a time of great upheaval and adjustment, as two become three. However, your relationship as a couple is still very important. Communication and time for each other will help you both as you adjust to your new role as parents.

Many women struggle with dividing their attention between their partner and their baby, particularly in the early weeks. You may feel that it takes all your time to look after your baby and yourself, and you don't have any time or energy to give to your partner. You may find that at times you don't want your partner near you at all, as the baby is the focus of all your love and affection. If you feel like this it is really important to be able to talk it through together.

Dads can often feel pushed out, particularly if there are lots of women around when you first come home from hospital. During the day you may have grandmothers, midwives or health visitors in and out of your house; one dad commented to me that it sometimes felt like a Mothers' Union meeting! Again, it's important to make time to listen to your partner about how he is feeling, and how he would like to be included.

Bonding with Your Baby

A great emphasis has been placed on bonding with your baby in recent years, and many parents worry about whether this will happen immediately. Most parents feel a huge rush of love when they see their baby for the first time, and birth really is an amazing experience. However, not every parent feels this overwhelming sense of love when they first see their baby. Don't worry if this happens to you, as bonding is simply about the baby and parents getting to know each other, and your love for your baby will deepen over a period of time.

As a mum, you may feel you don't have a 'natural' love for your baby instantly, particularly if you have had a very traumatic delivery and birth. If your baby was premature or you had to have an emergency delivery, you may feel unprepared and shocked at the sudden arrival of this new person in your life. If you are very tired after delivery and want the midwives to take your baby for a little while, do ask them to do this, and don't feel guilty. Try not to worry about your feelings, as you are very likely to want to hold and feed your baby after you have had some sleep.

Once you are home, make the most of these precious early weeks to get to know your baby. Feed times are a great opportunity to cuddle your baby close, look into his eyes and talk to him. As he begins to gaze back at you and respond to your voice, you may feel bowled over by your growing love for him. You can also bond with your baby as you change, bath and dress him, chatting to him and cuddling him as you become confident in caring for him.

Dads also need to be part of the learning process in bonding with their baby. If the baby is breastfed, dads will not be able to be involved with feeding, but can still have special time with her. They can wind her, change her and bath her, as well as giving her lots of cuddles. Dads are often really good at settling babies in their cots after a feed.

Visitors

It is lovely to have friends and family come to visit you after your baby is born, as it is quite natural to want to show your new baby off. However, having too many visitors, especially in the early days, can leave you feeling absolutely exhausted. In general it is a good idea to have just a few visitors at a time, perhaps one or two each day. If you are feeling very tired then it's all right to have a few days without any visitors so that you and your partner can catch up.

If you are feeling overwhelmed by visitors, your partner or a good friend can answer the telephone and the door for a few days and explain to visitors that you are tired. Most people will understand that there are times you need to be on your own with your partner and other children. Similarly, you could put a notice on the door saying, 'Mother and baby resting – no visitors today, please.' If you are resting or feeding, don't feel guilty about taking the telephone off the hook for an hour or so.

When you do have visitors, remember that you don't have to make endless cups of tea and cakes for everyone. Show them where the kettle is and let them make you a cup of tea. If friends and family want to help in the early weeks, encourage them to bring a hot meal round once a day. Your wider family will probably want to come and see the new baby fairly soon after he's born. Do try to make time for family, but it's all right if you don't want them all to move in at once! Often you'll find your wider family are good at helping with other children, taking them out for walks or doing the shopping. Usually, the family will want to help out in any way they can, so don't be afraid to ask.

One of my clients said to me after her house was filled with flowers, 'Why can't somebody just bring me a cooked ham instead of flowers?' It is true: food is such a practical present when you've just had a baby. Gift baskets of food are a great idea; for example, there is a wonderful shop in London (the Beverly Hills Bakery) which delivers baskets of delicious muffins and cookies across the UK.

Your Physical Needs

Rest

After your baby has been born you will find that you really do need to rest. Whether you have had a fairly straightforward quick delivery, a long complicated one, a hospital or a home birth, you will be tired and your body will need rest. Some women feel 'high' and find it hard to switch off in the early days after birth. After my third child was born, I was very high and unable to sleep for several days. If you are finding it difficult to sleep, you will probably find that after a few days when you know you can relax with your baby, your sleep pattern improves and you sleep really deeply.

My gynaecologist said to me after our first baby was born, 'Rest for six weeks, eat well, and you won't look back.' This did pay off, but I know it is much easier with a first baby. When our third baby was born, I came out of hospital after six hours, and went straight home to run the farmhouse. Consequently I was very ill, bled heavily, and had to take to my bed. It is important not to try to get back to 'normal' life straight away. It is tempting to get up and get on, but in my experience if you do this too early, you may find you have no energy and are actually less able to cope.

If you are very tired in the early days, don't feel you have to hurry in the mornings, especially if you don't have other children. I often advise mums to go back to bed whenever they can. It's a good idea to go back to sleep after the early morning feed, nap again in the afternoon and sleep before the last feed at night if you need to. You will find that breastfeeding makes you very sleepy, and by the end of a feed you may well feel like dropping off. Try feeding your baby on the bed with your feet up so that you are resting while you feed. After the feed, you can tuck her in and go back to bed.

Nutrition

After your baby is born, you may find that you lose your appetite initially. You will find that this gradually comes back, and it can help to have some of your favourite foods to tempt you. You may find you have a real craving for sweet things, particularly if you are breastfeeding, so allow yourself a big slice of chocolate cake if you fancy it. You need an extra 600 calories per day if you are breastfeeding to help your milk production. Have a good, balanced diet and aim to have at least one proper meal during the day, as well as having healthy snacks while feeding. It's important to make sure that your fluid intake is good, as this will also help increase your milk supply. Have plenty to drink, including water, juices or hot drinks – whatever you like. If you are bottle feeding, it is still important to eat well to help your body recover from pregnancy and birth.

Looking After Your Body

Most women have some bruising and soreness in their perineal area after giving birth. Having plenty of hot baths with a few drops of lavender oil can help to soothe and heal this area. There are some good homeopathic remedies for reducing swelling, including arnica. If you have had stitches, you may find that ice packs soothe the wounds, and it can help to have a rubber ring to sit on to relieve pressure. You may find that it's uncomfortable to pass urine, and to ease the stinging you can pour a jug of warm water over your perineum as you do so. You may also find that you're quite frightened of having your bowels open for the first time after the birth, and it helps to eat plenty of fibre and fruit to avoid straining.

Blood loss is normal in the first few weeks after birth, but varies from woman to woman. If you find that you are passing large clots, or have severe pain in your stomach or flu-like symptoms, speak to your midwife or health visitor. Infections are not uncommon after giving birth, but can be easily treated with antibiotics.

If you've had a Caesarean section you will find that moving about will be difficult initially, as you will be sore and tender around your scar area. A section is major surgery, and you will be very tired as you recover, particularly if you had a long labour first. It will take you longer to get in and out of bed, and bending over the cot can be quite uncomfortable. You will need to find a comfortable feeding position, using pillows to support your baby so that he doesn't press on your scar. You may find that pushing the buggy or pram gives you a pain in the stomach, so as much as possible, get somebody else to push. Usually, your scar will heal quite quickly, but if you find that it is red and inflamed, do talk to your health visitor.

After birth, your stomach may still look quite big and you may worry that it hasn't gone down at all. Your figure will come back, but it's important to give yourself time and recognize that it takes longer for some mums than others. If you are breastfeeding, you will have 'after-pains', which feel like bad period pains. These are stimulated by the release of the hormone oxytocin when feeding and are a good sign, as they show that your uterus is contracting and beginning to go back to its former shape.

Night sweats are very common in the early weeks, and are caused by changing hormone levels after birth. Night sweats can make you feel as if you have flu, and you may wake several times in the night, covered in perspiration. If you do suffer from night sweats, the best thing to do is to get up, have a wash or shower and change your nightclothes.

Exercise

It is a good idea to have a little walk each day if you are feeling like it, but don't do any more than you feel you can. Often, just getting outside in the fresh air even for half an hour will do you good. Even in the winter, it's worth wrapping up and going out for a walk, as it can really give you a lift. Gentle exercise will help you regain your figure, but don't do any strenuous exercise until after your postnatal check-up.

Try to do your pelvic floor exercises when you can, as they pay off later on in life: many women who haven't done them suffer with stress incontinence later. Your midwife or physiotherapist will teach you what to do. You can do pelvic floor exercises whenever you think about them: when you are standing at the sink, or sitting in your car at the traffic lights.

Your Emotional Needs

Thinking About Your Birth Experience

You may find it helpful to talk about your birth experience, particularly if it was not what you had expected or planned for. It's quite natural to be preoccupied with your labour and delivery, and to want to share it with other people in the early days after birth. You might also find it helpful to write the experience down. After I had our babies I wrote my birth story, describing my feelings and the whole experience, and I'm sure this was a help to me in the early weeks. It has also been good to read them through again as I write this book.

'Me Time'

After your baby is born, it's very easy to focus completely on her and forget about your own personal needs. It's important to have daily time out for relaxation, even if it's just half an hour for a hot bath, reading a chapter of a good book or listening to some music. Try to treat yourself to something you really enjoy when you feel like going out again, perhaps going to the hairdresser or having a massage.

It's very easy to become isolated when you have a new baby, particularly if you don't have close friends or family living nearby. When you feel ready, going out to the shops or for a coffee will help to bring a sense of normality to life with your new baby. Going out for the first time can be quite scary on your own; I suffered with panic attacks when going out shopping after our two daughters were born. I did get through them, but it was a nasty experience, mostly due to hormonal changes in my body. It can help you to feel confident if someone goes with you, perhaps your partner, a family member or a friend. Once you are ready to go out more regularly, postnatal or NCT classes, breastfeeding groups and baby and toddler groups can be a good place to meet other parents. You may find that you establish some very good friendships as your babies grow up together.

Support at Home

Fathers can be invaluable in supporting and caring for both mother and baby in the early days at home. You will be much better able to rest if your partner can make you tea or breakfast in bed, or take the baby for a walk. If your partner is able to help keep the home clean and tidy, it will let you feel more relaxed. As your baby gets older, your partner could sometimes give your baby a feed during the night to enable you to have a full night's sleep. As new parents, both of you will be tired, so it's important that you can also call on other people to support you around the home.

Dads' Needs

Although your partner hasn't physically been through labour, he is likely to be exhausted, as supporting you in labour can be very emotionally draining. Once you are both home, your partner will also need to rest and catch up on lost sleep. In the early days, it will be very special for him to spend time getting to know your baby, cuddling him, changing him and maybe giving him his first bath at home.

In the first few weeks, your partner may be back at work, and broken nights can make him very tired. I often advise that there is no point in both parents being up in the night, and if mum is happy to do the majority of night feeds this will enable dad to cope during the day. Be aware that your partner will need time out too, and he may want to switch off for a while by reading or going out with some friends for an hour or so.

Time as a Couple

When you first come home from hospital, you will find that you have some special times together marvelling over your wonderful new baby. As you adjust to your new role as parents, it is important to be sensitive to each other's needs and make time to listen to each other. Even though you may not make love for some time after the birth, it is important to have cuddles and to share intimate times together. As much as possible, keep your sense of humour and be patient with each other in your physical relationship.

Coping in Difficult Circumstances

Life doesn't always work out as planned, and you may find that your baby is born while you are trying to cope with illness, bereavement, separation or divorce. Try to organize some help before you have your baby, so that somebody is on hand for you when you come home. It is important to have as much support and help as possible when you're going through a difficult time as well as looking after a newborn baby. Your support network may not involve a partner, but family and friends can provide great practical and emotional help.

If you have experienced domestic violence or trauma before the baby's birth, or your own experiences as a young baby or child were very traumatic, you will need extra support. As well as family and friends, it's important that you make contact with professionals whom you can talk to and who can support you through the challenges of life with a newborn baby.

Things that Don't Matter

Give yourself permission to:

- *have a good cry*
- *walk around in your dressing gown all day*
- *not have an immaculately clean house*
- *not get the ironing done*
- *allow friends to do things around the house for you*
- *leave your baby in her sleepsuit all day*
- *go back to bed in the morning if you're tired*
- *feed in bed with your feet up*
- *express milk so that someone else can do a feed*
- *make some space to do things for yourself*
- *do your shopping online*
- *not go back to work immediately*
- *take time to get back to normality*
- *have realistic expectations about your body's recovery*
- *give your tummy time to return to pre-pregnancy size.*

Becoming a parent is a huge change in your life, and I often advise parents to try not to worry about how they feel and the difficulties when they first come home. Just remember, it's not forever. It really will pass and you will feel normal again. If you have a bad day, put it behind you and start again tomorrow.

CHAPTER 4

General Care of Your Baby

Most parents feel overwhelmed by the responsibility of caring for a newborn baby when they first come home from hospital. This is perfectly normal, and you will find that your initial fear passes as you get to know your baby, and become confident in how to look after him. The vast majority of parents I've worked with feel that their antenatal classes have prepared them well for pregnancy and birth, but left them quite unprepared for bringing their baby home. I hope this chapter will guide you in the practical aspects of baby care, particularly if this is your first child and you haven't had much experience of babies.

General Baby Care, Nought to Six Months

This first section outlines how to care for newborns and young babies up to six months. The second section looks at how to look after your baby from six to twelve months as she grows and develops.

How to Hold and Handle Your Baby

When your baby is very tiny, it can feel quite scary to pick him up, as he seems so fragile. However, he will feel much more secure if you pick him up confidently and hold him in a secure, firm way. To pick him up, put one hand under his head and neck, supporting his head firmly, and the other hand under his body. Lift him up towards you and place his head securely in the crook of your arm. Support his body with your arm underneath him, bringing the other arm around for extra support.

When you feel more confident, you can rest your baby's body against yours with her head either facing over your shoulder or resting on your chest (see below). In these positions, make sure you support her head and neck firmly with your free arm. You can also lay your baby across your lap on her tummy, which many babies love, especially if they have wind. Make sure your legs are at a slight angle so that your baby can't roll off onto the floor. Once your baby can support her head (usually by about three months), you will find you are both much more confident, and you can hold her in lots of different positions.

If you have other children, make sure that they understand how to hold the baby carefully and securely. Don't let young children pick the baby up when you're not in the room to supervise. When friends or family visit, don't be afraid to show them how you like him to be picked up and held: you're the expert.

Before dressing your baby, always make sure she has her nappy on first. Young babies will usually need a vest on underneath their sleepsuit or day clothes, unless the weather is really hot. If the temperature is high at night, your baby may only need a vest on. The most practical baby clothes allow easy access to your baby's nappy for changing. Nighties are a good option for sleeping in as they make changing easier at night. Make sure that vests have poppers between the legs and sleepsuits have poppers all the way down the front and legs. As your baby grows, she will need the next size of clothes so that she's not uncomfortable.

Putting on a Vest

- *Lie your baby down on his changing mat, the bed or floor.*
- *Open the vest poppers.*
- *Open the envelope neck as wide as you can.*
- *Put the whole vest over his head.*
- *Put your hand into the sleeve with your fingers right through.*
- *Take hold of your baby's hand and thread it through the sleeve.*

- *Keep your baby's fingers covered with your hand so that they don't catch.*
- *Repeat with the other sleeve.*
- *Bring the long side of the vest down under his back and match up the poppers between his legs.*

Putting on a Sleepsuit

- *Open all the poppers of the sleepsuit.*
- *Lay the sleepsuit out on the changing mat, bed or floor.*
- *Lay your baby in the middle of the sleepsuit.*
- *Use one hand to gather up the sleeve.*
- *Take hold of your baby's hand with your other hand and thread it through the sleeve.*
- *Repeat with the other sleeve.*
- *Gather up the leg of the sleepsuit.*
- *Take hold of your baby's foot and gently ease it into the leg.*
- *Pull the fabric up over your baby's leg.*
- *Repeat with the other leg.*
- *Match up the poppers from the top down.*

To put on a cardigan or jacket use the same method, threading your baby's hand through the sleeve carefully. For all-in-one suits, use exactly the same technique as for sleepsuits.

Changing and Washing Baby Clothes

Babies' clothes should be changed fairly regularly, but not necessarily every day. I usually advise that you put on a clean vest each day, but a sleepsuit may last you two days. If your baby has been very sick or had a leaky nappy, she will need a change of clothes. It is important to have plenty of clean muslin squares or bibs, especially if your baby brings up a lot of milk.

Most baby clothes can go in the washing machine, and don't need a really hot wash. Washing at 40 °C or below is usually fine, but do read the label. Baby clothes can go in with your family's washing as well, as long as you use a non-biological washing powder, which is better for a baby's sensitive skin. You can tumble-dry or air-dry baby clothes, and it isn't essential to iron them. Clothes should be thoroughly dry and aired before you put them away.

How Often Will My Baby Need Changing?
Your baby will need to have his nappy changed every time you feed him, which will be around six times a day. During the night feed, I usually advise that you only change his nappy if it is dirty, to avoid waking him up completely. If your baby does a poo when he is asleep, you do not need to change his nappy straight away, as he will be fine until the next feed. During the day, change him if his nappy is leaking or if he is uncomfortable in a dirty nappy.

Where Should I Change My Baby?
The best place to change a baby is on a surface which allows you to stand upright and not bend over. If you have a changing unit or a chest of drawers, make sure that it is at a good height for your back. If you have a strap for the changing unit, use it to keep your baby secure. Don't leave your baby unattended at any point when you are changing her on a raised surface. In the first few weeks she will be quite still when you are changing her; however, this won't last for long, and she can easily wriggle or roll and fall off.

You can use a changing mat on the floor or the bed, but both of these may be difficult if you have pelvic problems or if you are very sore after giving birth. If you are changing your baby on the floor, make sure that he's not likely to be trodden on. Lay a towel, muslin or disposable changing mat liner on the mat before you change your baby, to mop up any accidents.

How to Change a Nappy

- *Lie your baby on her back on her changing mat.*
- *Undo her vest and tuck it up out of the way.*
- *Open the nappy.*
- *If the nappy is dirty, wipe away poo from front to back with the nappy.*
- *Lift both her legs at the ankles with one hand.*
- *Take off her nappy and wrap it up well to contain any poo.*

- *Wash her bottom thoroughly with cotton wool and water from front to back.*
- *Dry her off with a towel.*
- *Let her bottom air-dry for a few minutes without the nappy on.*
- *Lift both her legs up together with one hand.*
- *Place the nappy under her bottom.*
- *If using barrier cream, put a little on at this stage.*
- *Do her nappy up.*
- *Leave two to three fingers' space at the waistband to ensure that it is not too tight.*
- *Put the dirty nappy in a nappy sack for disposal or nappy bucket for washing.*
- *Wash your hands.*

What Will a Normal Dirty Nappy Look Like?

Your baby's first dirty nappies will contain a dark, sticky tar-like substance called meconium, which is perfectly normal. If you are breastfeeding, your baby's poo will be loose, yellow-green and frothy, and may look a bit like grain mustard. A bottle-fed baby's poo will be firmer in texture, and will be yellow-brown and more smelly. As solids are introduced into your baby's diet, his poo will become more solid in texture and will change in colour depending on what he's eating.

How to Wash Your Baby

In the early days of your baby's life, you don't need to bath her every day, but she does need to be 'top and tailed'. Your baby's face, ears and neck will need a gentle clean each day, and keeping her bottom clean will help to prevent nappy rash. Your baby's skin is very delicate, and you don't need to use lots of soap in the early days. In fact, you can top and tail using just plain water.

Top and Tailing

When babies are small, I usually use cotton wool to wash their faces and bottoms. When your baby is a bit bigger, you can use cloths or sponges, making sure that you have a different sponge or cloth for face and bottom.

- *Use warm water to wash your baby's face.*
- *Make sure to wash well into the folds in his neck and around his ears.*
- *Dry his face and neck carefully with a soft towel.*
- *Wipe your baby's hands.*
- *Wash his bottom with cotton wool and warm water.*
- *Wipe from front to back.*
- *Ensure that the folds of skin in the groin are clean.*
- *Clean gently underneath the testicles in boy babies.*
- *For girl babies, clean the vulva gently but don't clean inside.*
- *Dry his bottom carefully.*
- *Leave his nappy off for a while to air-dry if you want to.*
- *You can put a tissue or baby wipe over a baby boy's penis so that he doesn't wee on the wall.*

If your baby has sticky or runny eyes, which are quite common after birth, wash them carefully with cooled boiled water, from the inner corner of the eye by the nose out towards the cheek. Use a separate piece of cotton wool for each eye. If the discharge from the eyes is thick and green, contact your health visitor or GP, who can take a swab and may prescribe drops if needed.

Caring for the Umbilical Cord
Clean the cord very gently with cotton wool and warm water and don't touch it too much. Cleaning won't hurt the baby, and the cord will drop off within five to ten days. If the cord is smelly or you have any concerns, talk to your midwife.

Bathing

Although bathing your baby once a day is not essential, it can become a relaxing part of her bedtime routine if you give her a bath in the evening. I usually advise parents to give a baby a bath before a feed, rather than afterwards. From four to six weeks old, your baby will be happy to lie with the nappy off before a bath, but it can be helpful to do a baby boy's vest up between the legs to prevent him weeing everywhere.

Fill up your baby bath; if you are using a regular bath, put just a few inches of water in the bottom. Use your elbow or a bath thermometer to make sure the water is the right temperature, so that it feels warm but not hot. The water temperature should be around 36 to 38 °C, if you are using a bath thermometer. Make sure that your bathroom is warm, as babies can get chilly quite quickly.

When bathing a baby, I usually sit on a chair by the bath and hold him on my lap. I start with him wrapped up in a towel to wash his face and hair. I then unwrap him and wash his body, finally rinsing him off in the bath. I have used this method over the years, as I've found that many babies dislike having their clothes taken off, and seem to feel more secure and comfortable being in close contact with you while being bathed.

Washing Your Baby's Face and Hair

- *Make sure you have cotton wool, shampoo and liquid soap ready.*
- *Undress your baby and take off her nappy.*
- *Wrap her up securely in a towel with her arms by her sides.*
- *Hold your baby on your lap.*
- *Clean your baby's face.*
- *Use screwed-up cotton wool to clean her nose and ears.*
- *Tuck your baby under your arm and hold her over the bath.*
- *Use a little bathwater to wet her hair.*
- *Put a tiny drop of shampoo on her head and lather carefully.*
- *Rinse her hair thoroughly over the bath.*
- *Towel dry her face and hair.*

Washing Your Baby's Body

- *Unwrap the towel from around your baby, and lay him on your lap.*
- *Wash under his arms, chin and all over his body with liquid soap and water on your hands.*
- *Turn your baby towards you and wash his back in the same way.*

- Rinse your hands so they are not slippery.
- Put your arm under your baby's head and hold his arm securely.

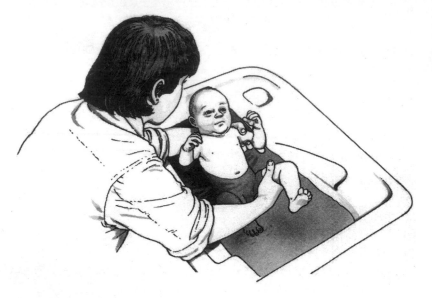

- Place your baby in the bathwater.
- Hold your baby securely in the water and rinse him with your free hand.
- Lift him out and wrap him securely in a towel.
- Dry your baby carefully on your lap.
- Turn him on his tummy to dry his back and creases in bottom and legs.
- Massage him with moisturising cream or baby oil (optional).

When you are rinsing your baby in the bath, don't keep her in too long as she can get cold very quickly. I usually advise that you don't use any bubble bath in the water for about the first month. If your baby's skin is very dry, you can use a drop or two of olive oil or baby oil in the bath. Be careful, as she will be very slippery if you use oil! If you like baby powder, use it quite sparingly, as it can make her cough if she breathes it in. It is a good idea to shake some powder on your hand first, and then apply it to your baby.

Cutting Your Baby's Fingernails

Some babies are born with long fingernails, which is quite normal. This often means that they scratch themselves accidentally. You only need to cut your baby's fingernails when they are long. Use a special pair of baby nail scissors with rounded ends, and cut your baby's nails straight across. Babies' fingers can bleed quite easily, so be as careful as you can.

Caring for Your Baby's Penis if He Has Been Circumcised

Some parents choose to have their baby circumcised for social, traditional or religious reasons. However, there is no medical evidence that circumcision is needed to keep the penis clean. If your baby has been circumcised, clean the area gently with cotton wool and warm water, and be aware that it could be sore for the first few days after circumcision. It's fine for your baby to have a bath once the area begins to heal.

How to Get Your Baby Ready to Go Out

As soon as you feel ready to take your baby out for little walks, go for it! Outings are great for you, as you can get out of the house and see friends again. Your baby will enjoy going out, as he will love the movement of his pram or buggy, and it is good for him to have fresh air. You may feel quite daunted by the whole idea of going out with a new baby, and lots of mothers I've worked with do feel like this, particularly if they have had a difficult delivery. I often advise new mothers to take a short first trip, even just to the shops. It can help to have your partner or a friend with you to give you confidence.

A good tip is to make sure you have plenty of time to get ready to take your baby out. You will be surprised how much time it takes to assemble all the bits and pieces you might need for your outing. Gather the things you need after a feed whilst your baby is happy in her cot or sitting in her chair.

Checklist: What Do I Need for an Outing?

- *Make sure your pram or buggy is ready (either folded down for the car, or assembled if you are walking from home).*
- *Take a raincover or sunshade if needed.*

- *Put together your changing bag:*
  clean nappies
  nappy sacks
  baby wipes
  change of clothes
  two muslin squares.
- *Make up a bottle of formula (if bottle feeding).*
- *Alternatively, take a bottle of boiled water with formula to add.*
- *If taking bottles, make sure to put them in an insulated bag to stay warm.*
- *Don't forget to pack your handbag with the things you need.*

Once your pram or buggy is ready and your bags are packed, get your baby dressed to go out. If the weather is cold, make sure he has sufficient warm clothes on. In chilly weather he will need a hat, bootees, a jacket or all-in-one over his sleepsuit and maybe an extra blanket in his pram or buggy. If it is hot, make sure he's not overdressed, but he will need protecting from the sun with a hat and sunscreen. Cotton clothes are usually best for your baby in the heat. Once your baby is dressed, put him in the pram, buggy or car seat, and you're ready to go.

Safety in the Home

Babies under six months of age don't normally move around very much, but there are a number of things to consider to make sure your baby is safe and secure at home.

Safety Indoors

If you don't already have smoke alarms fitted in your home, make sure you have them fitted before your baby arrives. Babies are very susceptible to lung damage from breathing in smoke, so check that all smoke alarms are working properly before you bring your baby home from hospital. Cigarette smoke is also very harmful to babies, so it's important that you and any visitors to your house do not smoke around the baby. If you or any visitors do smoke, try to ensure that this is outside the house.

Young babies cannot regulate their own body temperature very well, so make sure that your home is not too hot or cold. Ideally, the temperature in your baby's room should be 16 to 18 °C. Make sure you don't leave your baby in a draught, as she can get cold quite quickly.

Many newborn babies stay quite still on a changing mat; however, they soon become more wriggly. It's very important not to leave your baby alone on a changing mat, as he can easily wriggle off and fall. Your baby can lie safely in the middle of your bed until he can roll over, but keep an eye on him as once he can move about it's surprising how quickly he can reach the edge. When your baby is sitting in a chair, strap him in to prevent him slipping out, and never put a bouncy chair on a high surface.

Safety Outdoors
If your baby is having a sleep outside, you will need a cat net or insect net for the pram to protect her. If you have pets, make sure that they can't jump up onto the baby or knock her pram over. You will also need to protect your baby from the elements, with a sunshade and sunscreen in hot weather, and a raincover in wet weather. I often advise parents not to be worried about taking their baby outdoors in the rain; as long as you have a raincover and your baby is warm enough, she will be quite happy.

Safety during Play
You will probably receive lots of toys as presents for your baby. With any toys you buy or are given, make sure they have the CE safety mark and are appropriate for your baby's age. As he gets older and starts putting everything in his mouth, make sure that toys don't have small parts or ribbons he could choke on. Also ensure that your baby can't get hold of older children's toys or small objects around the house and put them in his mouth.

Your baby will need a safe place to play, where older children or pets won't fall over her. If you have room, a playpen is a great idea and your baby can go into it from about six weeks of age. If your baby gets used to a playpen fairly early in life, you will probably find that she feels quite happy in it, as it's established as her own play area. If you don't have space for a playpen, an activity mat with raised sides or an area of floor surrounded by cushions works just as well. If you're doing things near your baby's bedroom, you can also put your baby in her cot to play.

General Baby Care, Six to Twelve Months

Holding Your Older Baby

By six to twelve months your baby will be heavier, and more able to wriggle about in your arms. You will need to hold your baby very securely when picking her up and carrying her. Take care of your back, particularly when you lift her in and out of her cot, or pick her up from the floor. It's tempting to walk around with your baby on your hip a lot, but this can hurt your back. Also, if you try to avoid always carrying your baby around, she will have more opportunities to practise crawling and walking.

Once your baby is learning to walk, he will initially need some support to prevent him toppling over. You can hold both his hands and encourage him to walk towards you, or hold him around his middle to give him stability.

Clothing for the Older Baby

As your baby gets older, it's nice to have more variety in her wardrobe. She will only need a sleepsuit at night, and you may find that tops and trousers are most practical during the day as she begins to crawl around and get dirty knees. It's worth having some trousers in hard-wearing fabrics once your baby is crawling; however, you will find that your baby grows out of things quite quickly at this stage.

Before your baby is walking, he can wear soft baby shoes, but his feet will have the best conditions to grow if they are bare. Make sure his feet don't get cold, and put socks or bootees on in colder weather. Your baby doesn't need proper hard-soled shoes until he is walking. When you buy his first pair of shoes, take him to a good shoe shop to have his feet measured, and staff there will be able to advise you.

When you take your baby out, she won't need to be wrapped up in lots of blankets as she gets older. She will probably be warm enough with a jacket or all-in-one suit. Once she is walking, she will really enjoy wet-weather outings, and will need a waterproof jacket and trousers, and a pair of wellington boots for splashing in puddles.

Nappy Changing

Your baby will still need his nappy changed at each feed or mealtime, and if he has a dirty nappy in between. Once he is eating solid food, you will find his dirty nappies will be more smelly and solid. If he has done a poo he will probably complain and want to be changed fairly quickly. Use a good barrier cream if you find he suffers from a sore bottom.

Nappy changing can become quite a challenge as your baby gets older, as she wriggles about and kicks more. It's quite normal at this age for your baby to shout and object to being changed. She may need some distraction when having her nappy changed, such as a small toy to play with.

Bathing and Washing

Once your baby is able to sit up, you probably won't want to be bathing him on your lap wrapped in a towel as you would for a newborn. You can put him in the bath in a special support or on a non-slip rubber mat, supporting his body with your arm. To wash his hair, lean your baby back over your arm and use your free hand to lather and rinse his hair. You can wash his body with your free hand, and rinse him off in the bathwater. Your baby does not need to have his hair washed every day, and twice a week is usually fine. However, once he is feeding himself you may find that he has food in his hair and it needs washing more often. Now that he's bigger he can spend longer in the bath as he won't get cold so quickly, and he will enjoy playing with toys or splashing in the water.

By the time your baby is a year old, it's a good idea to introduce a toothbrush and baby toothpaste. Your baby will need a lot of help with this, and you will have to hold her hand and direct her to her teeth. Don't worry if it's not a very thorough clean at this stage; you're just helping your baby learn about the routine of cleaning her teeth.

Never leave your baby alone in the bathroom, even when he can sit or stand up unaided. Babies can drown in a very small amount of water, and can very easily slip in the bath. Make sure you won't be distracted at bathtime, and ignore the telephone or doorbell.

Out and About

Older babies will enjoy a wider variety of outings and trips, and will be happy to stay out for longer periods. Your baby will be taking a lot more interest in his surroundings, and will especially enjoy looking at animals and visiting play areas designed for young children. You could meet up with a group of friends and their babies, which is good for your baby's developing social skills and good fun for you too. Most babies really enjoy swimming, and you can take your baby from an early age, as it's great exercise for both you and him.

You will still need to take a changing bag with you, and once your baby is eating solid food, don't forget to take this too. By the time she is a year old, you may want to have some finger food and drinks with you. If she is walking, you may want to take a pair of baby reins with you, which will help you to keep her safe, particularly in crowds or busy traffic.

In hot weather, you will need a hat and sunscreen for your baby and a sunshade for the buggy. When travelling in hot weather, it's important never to leave your baby in the car unattended, as he can overheat very quickly. In wet weather, remember to take the cover for the buggy and any wet-weather clothing your baby needs.

Safety in the Home

As your baby becomes increasingly mobile and curious, you will find that you have lots to think about in terms of safety around the home. However, it is easy to be over-protective and get very anxious about safety. I feel one of the most important things is to have a balance, so that your baby can be free to discover and explore her surroundings, but kept safe from real dangers.

Safety Indoors

As soon as your baby is crawling, you will need stairgates to prevent him from trying to go up or down the stairs and falling. You may also want to have a gate to prevent him from crawling or walking into the kitchen or other rooms where you want to keep the door open. If you have a fire, you will also need a fireguard which goes right around to prevent him getting close. When your baby is in a highchair or pushchair, he will need to be strapped in, as he can easily get out once he is mobile.

Your baby can reach out for things, and will be becoming more dextrous, so it's important to keep out of her reach anything that can cause her harm. Keep saucepan handles, kettle and iron flexes away from the edge of surfaces so that she can't pull them down onto herself and get scalded or burned. Make sure she is kept away from the stove and any hot food and drinks. Make sure she can't reach out for any sharp objects or heavy items that could fall on her.

You can buy a range of safety items to protect your baby. Socket protectors are a good idea to prevent him putting his fingers into electrical sockets, and door and cupboard latches protect him from trapping his fingers or pulling things out of cupboards. You can also buy corner protectors for tables to prevent bumps and knocks when your baby is learning to walk.

Your baby will love to explore by putting things into her mouth. Make sure you wash her hands before she eats; however, you don't need to keep washing her hands while she is playing. Your baby will get dirty hands when she's crawling and walking around, and will put her fingers in her mouth. Try not to worry about this, as exposure to some dirt will build her immunity. However, it is important to keep her highchair and eating utensils clean.

If your baby does put something in his mouth and chokes on it, hold him stomach-down over your arm, with his head towards the floor, and tap him sharply several times between the shoulder blades. This should dislodge the item from his windpipe. If your baby swallows any object, you need to contact your doctor. Always make sure that any kitchen or bathroom cleaners are kept locked away from your baby. If he has ingested any cleaning chemicals, go straight to the hospital or contact an ambulance.

Safety Outdoors

Your baby will enjoy playing in the garden as she gets older; however, she will need you to be nearby to keep an eye on her. She will tend to make a beeline for anything dirty or anything with water in it, so try to put out of reach anything that can cause real harm. If you have pets, make sure that feeding bowls are out of the way and any poo is removed before your baby plays in the garden.

If you have a pond or water feature, make sure that it is fenced off or has a protective cover, as babies can drown easily even in very shallow water. Make sure that poisonous plants are not within reach, as your baby will probably test out what leaves and flowers taste like. Watch what he puts in his mouth, as he can easily choke on little stones or nuts from trees. Have some anti-histamine cream or Piriton liquid in your cupboard in case he is stung or bitten by insects.

Safety during Play

Your baby will have a greater variety of toys as she gets older. Again, make sure they have a CE safety mark and are suitable for her age. It's a good idea to wash her toys every now and again, as she will be putting them in her mouth. You can put some plastic toys in the dishwasher, and some soft toys can go in the washing machine.

If your baby is still happy in his playpen, it is a good place for him to be; however, you may find he wants to explore further and shouts when he's in it. While he is playing and exploring, make sure that your baby can't get hold of things that could harm him. You can either approach this by putting things out of reach, or giving him a firm 'No!' when he has reached for something he shouldn't have.

Your baby will enjoy copying you and playing with 'grown-up' things. Obviously, make sure that she hasn't got hold of anything unhygienic such as the toilet brush, or unsafe such as a kitchen knife. You can give her household objects to play with, such as a wooden spoon or plastic box, but always make sure that she can't cause herself any real harm with them.

As your baby grows and develops, you will need to set new boundaries about what he can and can't do safely. Allowing your baby to explore and have new experiences will help him to become a more confident child.

CHAPTER 5

Feeding Your Baby

During your pregnancy, one of the main things you will need to decide is how you are going to feed your baby – is it going to be breast or bottle? It's a good idea for you and your partner to talk this through and decide before your baby is born. If you're having a hospital delivery, you also need to tell the staff which method you are planning to use.

Breast or Bottle? Making Your Choice

Breastfeeding is very popular today for all sorts of reasons. First of all, it is very good for the baby as breast milk is full of antibodies, which help to protect against infection and illness. Infections such as gastroenteritis are unlikely to occur in breastfed babies. Breast milk is always sterile, and it's the perfect food for your baby as it's easy for her to digest. It also helps to protect against allergies such as eczema and asthma. It is more difficult to overfeed your baby when breastfeeding. It's good for you too and helps you to regain your figure, as it uses up plenty of extra calories. Breastfeeding is very satisfying, and helps you to bond with your baby. It also usually delays your periods starting again; however, this is not a foolproof method of contraception. Breastfeeding can be easier, as you have no bottles to sterilize, and it's cheaper as well. You can express your milk so that your partner or other people can be involved in feeding your baby too.

I would recommend to all mothers that they try to breastfeed in the first instance even if it's just for a few weeks. Having said that, many babies today are bottle fed. If you are not able to breastfeed, or choose not to, don't worry. You can bond with your baby through bottle feeding in the same way as with breastfeeding.

Bottle feeding enables you to know how much milk your baby is having. As with expressed breast milk, bottle feeding allows other people, including siblings, to be involved with feed time. Formula milk takes longer to digest than breast milk, and some babies will sleep for longer between feeds. For you, bottle feeding requires less energy, and you will not have leaky breasts or sore nipples. Going back to work can be easier, as your baby is already used to feeding from a bottle. However, it is easier to overfeed your baby with a bottle, and this can make him more likely to be sick.

I always encourage mothers to have a go at breastfeeding, even if they find they have to give up for any reason. Breastfeeding may take between six and eight weeks to establish, so persevere! Many mothers give up too soon because they are not told that it can take time.

Breastfeeding

At the Birth

Normally, your baby will be handed to you to suckle as soon as she is born. Amazingly, as soon as the baby is put to you, she will usually turn her head to your nipple and begin to suckle. This is a wonderful built-in instinct. Make sure that the midwife helps you to get your baby 'latched on' properly. She needs to have her mouth wide open, with the nipple and areola (the dark area around the nipple) right in her mouth. To begin with, make sure that she does not suckle for too long, to minimize soreness.

It is very common for mothers to have tender nipples in the first few days, but feeding for a few minutes at a time will help to harden the nipples. Don't let your baby just suck on an empty breast indefinitely, as you will soon become sore. Suckling time can be increased over the next few days, until the baby is feeding for ten to twenty minutes on each breast. It's a good idea for your baby to feed on demand, little and often, during the first few days, as this will stimulate your milk supply.

Initially you will find that your milk is yellow and thin; this is called colostrum, and your baby will only take a little bit at a time. Around the third or fourth day, your milk will come in – this will be white and thin. The first milk is the foremilk, which quenches your baby's thirst. About two-thirds of the way through the feed on each breast, the baby will reach the hindmilk. The hindmilk is higher in fat and rich in calories, so it helps to keep your baby satisfied and full for longer between feeds.

Your breasts will be very full, and you may feel quite uncomfortable and hot. If your breasts are very hard and it's difficult for the baby to latch on, you can use warm flannels or have a warm bath and stroke your breast towards the nipple to express milk. To help stimulate your milk supply, it's a good idea to feed your baby from both breasts at each feed if you can. Empty one side completely, then offer the second breast to aid your comfort.

You will experience 'after-pains' like bad period pains when breastfeeding. This is because your baby's suckling stimulates your brain to produce a hormone called oxytocin, which causes your uterus to contract and shrink back to its pre-natal size. Oxytocin can also help you to relax and sleep, so it's well worth breastfeeding for the sake of your body as well as your baby's.

There are three main positions for breastfeeding. The basic one is for you to sit up and hold your baby in your arms with his head cradled in the crook of your arm and his tummy facing you. It often helps to put a pillow on your lap under your baby's body to bring him up to your breast, so that you don't have to lean over him. You may find that you get bad headaches if you regularly lean over when feeding. It's important to keep his body tucked closely into yours, and you can put your hand on his back to help support him. The other hand is then free to put your breast to him. He will usually turn his head towards your breast, and this is the right position for him to latch on. A nice way to remember this position is 'nose to nipple and tummy to mummy'.

I have affectionately termed position number two the 'rugby position'. Your baby's head is to your breast, and her body and legs are tucked through the crook of your arm behind you. Again, you can use a cushion to raise her body, making sure that her head is in the right position for latching on – nose to nipple. Use the hand of the supporting arm to hold her head, and your other hand is free to put your breast to her. This is an excellent position for twins, as you can feed them both at the same time. With both positions one and two, you can sit in an armchair or on the bed, preferably with your feet up to rest.

The third position enables you to lie in bed, so this is a great one for night feeds. Both you and your baby lie on your sides, maintaining the basic 'nose to nipple, tummy to mummy' position. You can place your hand on your baby's back to keep his body close to you, and lay your head on your pillow. Be aware that it's very easy to fall asleep in this position. If you find you are very sleepy during the night feed, perhaps try using one of the sitting positions instead.

It's a good idea to vary the position in which you feed your baby, as this helps to clear the milk ducts in different parts of the breast.

This is particularly helpful if you are suffering from engorged breasts. Whatever position you choose, make sure that your breast does not squash or cover your baby's nose, preventing her from breathing properly. This can happen particularly when your breasts are very full, so if you need to, gently move your breast away from her nose. If you have had a Caesarean section, it's very important to be comfortable when feeding, so use a pillow to take the pressure off your stomach.

Latching on and off the Breast

Before you begin to feed your baby, it's always important to wash your hands. Once you've decided which position to feed your baby in, turn his head towards your breast. Normally, he will make a

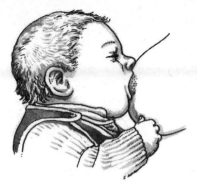

'rooting' face. This is where he opens and closes his mouth and turns his head round to find your nipple. Make sure his mouth is wide open and hold your breast, putting the whole nipple and areola right into his mouth. You will know by the feel of this whether he has latched on properly or not. If you feel as if he's biting on the nipple and a lot of the areola is showing, he has probably not latched on properly. If this happens, take him off and start again. To take him off, gently put your little finger into the corner of his mouth to break the seal, and ease his mouth open. You can then take your nipple out and latch him on again, making sure that his mouth is really open wide. Never pull your baby off the breast, as it will not only hurt you but will be uncomfortable for him too. After a few feeds you will get to know when he's latched on properly; however, be aware that it is normal for latching on and let-down of milk to be quite uncomfortable initially. As your nipples harden up this will become easier.

If your baby is very sleepy it can be more difficult to encourage her to latch on. You can change her nappy to wake her up before feeding, but if she is still sleepy there are a few techniques you can try. Tickle her on the cheeks and under the chin as you put her to your breast, gently squeeze out some milk and put that to her mouth. Usually as she gets the taste of the milk, she will want to start feeding and will begin rooting and opening her mouth. Sometimes stroking her top lip will encourage her to open her mouth. At that stage you can put her onto the breast. If she becomes sleepy after just a few sucks, you can gently blow on her face or tickle her neck and feet to wake her up again. These methods usually work, but if she is really too sleepy to feed, don't worry. Tuck her down and leave her for a while and then try again.

Let-down and Feeding

Before you start to feed, you will notice that your breasts are very full and may leak milk, particularly first thing in the morning. You may

63

also find that this happens when you hear your baby crying and a feed is due.

Once your baby is latched on, you will normally find that he has a good strong suck. As you relax, you will feel a tingling sensation, which means that 'let-down' is happening (your milk is flowing). You can tell that he's feeding because you can see his jaw moving and hear him swallowing. You will find that he does this for several minutes, and as breastfeeding becomes more established he will suck like this for longer periods. You will usually find that as you feed your other breast will leak; this is quite normal, but a bit of a nuisance.

Your baby will usually take most of her feed in the first eight to ten minutes of suckling. Sometimes your baby will come off the breast naturally, and this means she is ready to be winded. If she doesn't, then when her sucking begins to slow down and she appears to lose interest, unlatch and wind her. When your baby has wind, she may squirm and pull away from the breast during feeding. She may also look quite uncomfortable and even cry. If you have a lot of milk, and think your baby may have wind, unlatch and burp her.

When he is winded, put him back on again on the same breast if you still have milk there. If your baby has emptied this breast, he will soon let you know by being frustrated when you put him back. In the early days, feed your baby from the other side after winding so that you are stimulating milk flow in both breasts. The more your baby sucks, the more milk you will produce. Once your milk has come in properly, you will probably find that one breast is enough for your baby at one feed, and you can begin the next feed with the other breast.

At some feeds, babies will seem very hungry and have a longer feed, whereas the next one may be shorter. Babies tend to be extremely hungry when they have growth spurts, at about three days, three weeks, six weeks and three months of age. You may find that they wake earlier and have bigger feeds around these times, and this is perfectly normal. Some babies will empty a breast in around ten minutes, whereas others are happy to feed for twenty to forty minutes.

Winding

I feel that winding is an important part of feed time, and not to be underestimated. Winding means to help your baby to burp, to bring up any air that has gone into her stomach while feeding. If a baby is not winded properly it can prevent her from having a good feed, and if she's not been able to feed she will not settle to sleep well. Also, if she's fed on top of wind she will often be very sick. Usually babies need to be winded halfway through their feed, and then again at the end, but some babies need winding at frequent intervals during feeding. If mothers have a very rapid flow of milk, this can be as often as every two to three minutes.

There are a number of positions you can try to wind your baby. I usually start by sitting him up on your lap holding his back with one hand, with the other hand on his stomach. He needs to be facing to the side. Hold him close into your body so that he feels secure and quite firmly rub his back up and down while holding his stomach. This should make him burp. When babies are tiny, one burp may be enough, but some may need more than this. If this method doesn't work, put him on your shoulder with his head facing behind you, and quite firmly rub his back. Another position is to lie him on his stomach on your lap, with your legs slightly apart, and firmly rub his back. When you sit him up after this, he will often bring up his wind. If you're changing his nappy mid-feed, sit him upright after the nappy change and hold him under the chin. Again, rub his back firmly and you will find that this helps him to bring up his wind.

Movement is the key to bringing up wind, so you can change the position or walk around with your baby while winding her on your shoulder. As well as bringing up wind she may also 'posset', which means bringing up a little bit of milk. This is quite normal, and some babies bring up more than others. You're very fortunate if your baby doesn't bring up anything at all!

Your Milk Supply

Milk supply varies between mothers; some may struggle to produce enough, whereas others seem to produce gallons. If you have had a Caesarean section or if your baby was premature, your milk may take longer to come in. In hospitals today, babies are only fed formula milk if they are showing signs of hypoglycaemia, such as being jittery or cold. If your milk supply is low, there is no problem with giving a little formula to ease hunger, but keep putting your baby to the breast to stimulate milk supply.

It is very important to eat well when you're breastfeeding. You need an extra 600 calories a day to produce milk, so now's the time to enjoy cake and puddings. A good balanced diet will encourage a good milk supply. Eat plenty, and do snack, as you will find that you are very hungry when breastfeeding. In my experience, a glass of wine with an evening meal is fine, but champagne seems to give babies wind. I would also recommend that you avoid highly spiced foods unless they have been part of your everyday diet throughout pregnancy. Over the years I've seen fads come and go regarding which foods should and should not be eaten while breastfeeding. However, in general, my feeling is that what agrees with you will agree with your baby.

Your body has used a lot of energy to support your baby during pregnancy and take you through birth, so you need plenty of rest. Producing milk and getting up to feed in the night will also make you feel pretty tired, so make sure that you get as much rest as possible, particularly in the first month. Any anxiety or stress can prevent you from producing milk, so if at all possible have time to yourself to relax and be pampered.

Some medications should not be taken whilst breastfeeding. Check with your GP if you have any concerns about medication you are taking.

There are several reasons for expressing breast milk. You may have more milk than your baby needs, and need to express it to make your breasts more comfortable. However, be aware that expressing can increase engorgement, as your brain tells your body that you need to produce more milk. On the other hand, you may need to express in order to encourage your milk supply. If you are ill and unable to physically feed you may want to express. Expressing milk enables partners and others to be involved in feeding too, particularly if you are going back to work.

To express milk, you need a breast pump. These are either hand-operated or electric; I personally prefer the electric ones as they are quicker and easier to use. Breast pumps work by mimicking your baby's natural sucking action. You need to put the pump on, following the manufacturer's instructions, and allow time for your milk to let down. Holding your baby and relaxing will encourage let-down. It may take a little while when you first express milk, and the sensation can be quite strange.

If you're expressing milk so that your partner can help with the night feed it's a good idea to express earlier in the day (before about 2.00 p.m.), as your milk is at its best quality at this time. If you're expressing to relieve engorged breasts, express a little before each feed. To encourage milk supply, express a little milk after daytime feeds. If expressing excess milk for freezing, you can do this whenever you need to, but ensure that you haven't emptied your breast before a feed.

If you find that your other breast is leaking a lot of milk while you feed, you can buy breast shells to collect this milk. Put a sterilized breast shell gently inside your bra, making sure it doesn't press too hard on your breast. Always use breast shells with care, as they can block your milk ducts if used for too long or with too much pressure. Once you have stopped leaking, you can remove the breast shell and tip the milk collected into a sterilized bottle after the feed. The milk collected in breast shells is foremilk, so I wouldn't recommend using it as a top-up feed, but it can be mixed with other expressed breast milk.

Fresh breast milk can be kept in the fridge for twenty-four hours. Breast milk can be frozen in special bags and will keep for up to three months in the freezer. Sterilized freezer bags can be bought at any chemist, and will usually have a space for you to write the date the milk was expressed. To defrost milk, remove from the freezer in the bag and leave to thaw. If frozen milk is required immediately, you can place the bag in a jug of warm water.

Breastfeeding Twins

I advise mothers of twins to feed them together whenever possible. One mother of twins I have worked with commented that she didn't know how she would have managed, as she would have been feeding constantly had she not breastfed her twins at the same time. It is perfectly possible to breastfeed twins at the same time, using the 'rugby position' with one baby's body tucked under each arm. When twins are small, you can also use the regular breastfeeding

position, supporting each baby's head in the crook of your arm with one twin resting on top of the other. However, you may find this position uncomfortable if you have had a Caesarean delivery.

What if I Can't Breastfeed?

I can speak from personal experience about having to give up breastfeeding, and how difficult this was for me. When our first baby was born, I had lots of milk and enjoyed breastfeeding until I became very ill with mastitis, which was left untreated. Sadly, at this stage I had to give up. I was not encouraged to persevere with breastfeeding with our next two babies. I felt incredibly guilty and very sad about not breastfeeding, and it took me a long time to come to terms with. I believe that with the right help I would have been able to breastfeed all of our babies. My experience has led me to feel passionately that all mothers should have professional support and encouragement with breastfeeding, because normally it doesn't just happen.

There are some excellent breastfeeding counsellors nowadays, who will be only too happy to help you establish breastfeeding. In the UK, a local NCT group can put you in touch with a breastfeeding adviser who will come and visit you in your home. Midwives and health visitors are also a good source of information about breastfeeding support.

There may be circumstances in which you are unable to breastfeed, for example if you have had surgery or previous serious illness, or if you are taking medication. Your baby may not be able to feed from the breast if he was very premature, or if he has physical disabilities or illness. If for any reason you are unable to breastfeed, do not worry. Bottle-fed babies also do well. Your midwife will be able to advise you if there is a milk bank available in your area which can supply breast milk for you to bottle feed to your baby. The important thing is not to feel guilty. If you are struggling with this issue, talk about it to your midwife or doctor.

Problems with Breastfeeding

Sore Nipples

The most common problem with breastfeeding is sore nipples, usually resulting from babies not being latched on properly. If this goes on, your nipples will bleed, which is terribly painful and can result in infection leading to mastitis. You will also probably feel a lump in your breast and have a red mark. Prevention is certainly better than cure in this instance, so don't just grit your teeth and bear the pain. There are lots of different ways to deal with sore nipples. Wet nipples encourage soreness, so keep them as dry as possible. A current trend is to rub a little breast milk onto the nipple after the feed and allow this to dry naturally. One mother I have worked with used a hairdryer on the cool setting and this seemed to work. If possible, leave your breasts uncovered for about half an hour after the feed, as long as you're not leaking too much. Use breast pads for leakage, but make sure you change them at each feed to keep your nipples as dry and clean as possible. Sore nipples can also result from thrush infection; if you notice small white spots on your nipples you may have thrush (*candida albicans*), and this should be treated by your GP as it can be passed on to your baby.

Some people recommend that you prepare your breasts during pregnancy by rubbing creams into the nipples; however, everyone's skin is different, so you need to experiment with what works for you. Some mothers find that rubbing nipple cream on after a feed helps to soothe and harden the nipples. Read the label carefully, to see whether the cream needs to be washed off before the next feed. There are some good organic and non-fragranced creams on the market today. Don't wash your nipples with soap, as this can strip the natural oils from your skin.

If your nipples have cracked or become very sore, so that it's very painful to put your baby on the breast, I would recommend that you use nipple shields. I know that some health professionals do not like these because they may cause the baby to have more wind and your milk supply may decrease. However, in my experience some mothers have only been able to continue breastfeeding because they have used nipple shields. Use them with care, and as soon as you begin to heal take them off to allow your nipples to harden up again.

Engorged Breasts

Breasts can become engorged (very hard, and perhaps lumpy) quite early on in breastfeeding. This can be very uncomfortable, and your breasts may be painful to touch. The most important thing is to take a little milk out, either by suckling the baby or by expressing milk with a pump. If you express a lot of milk, this can give your body the message that you want your breasts to produce more, so just take enough off to be comfortable. When feeding, however, make sure that your baby empties or nearly empties the breast. This is the most natural way to reduce engorgement. A very good way to clear your milk ducts is to feed your baby in the 'rugby position' if you don't use this as your normal feeding position. Warm water will also soothe engorged breasts, so have a bath or use warm flannels to soften them and gently express some milk. If your breasts are engorged and the milk ducts are blocked, this does not necessarily mean you have mastitis.

Mastitis

Mastitis is an infection, and the first signs will be that you feel hot and sweaty as if you have flu coming on. You will also probably feel a lump in your breast and have a red mark. It is most important to be in touch with your doctor immediately if you think you have mastitis. Your doctor will prescribe antibiotics, and you can usually continue to breastfeed throughout the treatment. You will also need to take painkillers and make sure you drink lots of fluid.

Your Baby Will Suckle from a Bottle but Not from the Breast

You may have had to revert to bottle feeding your baby in the early days, but still want to breastfeed. If you find that your baby prefers to feed from a bottle, and makes a real fuss at the breast because she's desperately hungry, don't despair. Start by giving her about 25 ml (1 fl oz) of formula from the bottle, then hold her close to your breast, gently ease the teat out of her mouth and put your nipple in. You will normally find that this works, and she will begin to suck well at the breast. If you do this for two or three feeds, you will find that you can gradually dispense with the bottle and she will happily latch onto the breast.

Your Baby Won't Feed

You may find that your baby screams at the breast, and doesn't seem to be happy to feed at all. Wind him, as this is often the reason for crying. Sometimes your baby will seem distressed if he has emptied one breast and is still hungry. All you need to do is to put him on the other side, and you will usually find that he will settle down. Some babies are still hungry after both sides, in which case it is perfectly all right to top up with a bottle of formula – just try 25 ml (1 fl oz) to start with. He may be feeling unwell, and ear infections particularly cause discomfort in feeding. Babies can also get thrush infection in their mouths, which you may notice as little white spots. This makes it uncomfortable for him to feed. Contact your doctor if you are concerned about any illnesses affecting feeding.

It is important to keep as calm as possible with your baby if she is distressed during feed time. You can rock her and sing to help calm her, and stroke her head. Walking around with her on your shoulder can also help to settle her. Sometimes a fifteen-minute break before trying again helps both of you to feel calmer. If she is hungry, once she has settled to the breast and been fed you will find she is much more contented.

Anxiety

There are many reasons why you may feel anxious as a new mother, and this can affect milk supply and breastfeeding. Sleep deprivation can often exacerbate anxiety, so make sure you get as much rest as possible. The more relaxed you are, the more you will enjoy feed times, which helps your milk let-down. If you are very tired and have lots of things going on, you may find that your milk supply is not so good, especially in the evening. If this does happen, you can always top up your feed with a bottle.

Try to look forward to feed times as a special time for you and your baby. As you get to know him and bond with him, you will soon find yourself less anxious about feeding and looking after him.

Advice for Both Breast and Bottle Feeding

How Do I Know When My Baby Needs Feeding?

In the early days before you have established a feeding routine, you need to know when to feed your baby. At this stage your baby will be feeding 'on demand', which is ideal as it stimulates your milk supply and gives you lots of time to bond with your baby. Most of the time your baby will let you know that she is hungry by waking up, sucking her fingers or fist, rooting, turning her head from side to side and crying. She will sometimes start to stir about ten minutes before she actually wakes, and this is a sign that she is beginning to feel hungry. As a general rule, I would let her wake right up before you take her out of her cot, to enable her to come round naturally.

When you are beginning to set out a feeding routine (see Chapter 6), it's important to wake him for feed times during the day rather than waiting for him to wake naturally. If he wakes early for a feed you can turn him onto his other side and sometimes he will sleep for another half-hour or so. Alternatively, you can take him out for a little walk to settle him until the time you want to feed him. When he gets older and is beginning to take an interest in his surroundings, you can get him up and sit him in his chair to play. He will often be quite happy to sit for about twenty minutes watching the world go by. If he is desperately hungry and cannot be pacified, then by all means give him a good feed, and you will probably find that he sleeps until the next planned feed time.

How Do I Know When My Baby Has Had Enough?

You will soon be able to tell when your baby has finished her feed. Usually she will lose interest in sucking, and will either fall asleep or turn her head away and look around. It is very difficult to feed a baby who has really had enough! If you are not sure, I suggest having a ten-minute break and seeing how she responds after that. If she is starting to root or is fussing, try her on the breast or bottle again. If she still isn't interested then she's probably tired and ready for a sleep. When you tuck her down, if she won't settle, leave her for about ten minutes, and if she's still showing signs of hunger, give her a little bit more.

In the early days, you can check whether your baby is taking enough milk by making sure his nappies are wet. You may find it helps to put a tissue in the nappy, particularly with disposables, as they absorb a lot of liquid. He should have a wet nappy at each feed, and will often do a wee when his nappy is taken off. In general your baby should gain about 170–230 g (6–8 oz) a week for the first three months of life. If he is gaining weight at about this rate, then rest assured he is having enough.

The Environment for Feeding

It's important for both you and your baby to be comfortable when feeding. In the early weeks it's a good idea to feed with your feet up, so that you get as much rest as possible. The more relaxed you are, the easier it will be to begin to feed your baby, as she will be relaxed too. Before you begin to feed, wash your hands and have everything to hand that you'll need for feed time. This will help to avoid any disturbances for you or your baby. You will need:

- *a jug of water and a glass (you need to drink plenty if breastfeeding)*
- *snacks*
- *a bottle and warmer, if bottlefeeding or using expressed milk*
- *a changing mat*

- *a clean nappy*
- *cotton wool and a small bowl of warm water*
- *a nappy sack*
- *nappy rash cream (only necessary if his bottom is sore)*
- *clean breast pads if needed*
- *a muslin for any milk brought up*
- *a pillow or specialist feeding pillow.*

The room in which you are feeding should be warm and as quiet as possible. In the first few days, I would advise that you don't have the television on, and feel free to unplug the telephone. This reduces any disturbance to the feed and gives you time to bond with your baby. If you have other children, encourage them to play quietly sitting with you. It's important that siblings don't feel pushed out but are encouraged to be part of feed time, as long as they are gentle. Aim to have no visitors during feed times, particularly in the early days as this can take your concentration away from feeding. Don't feel bad if you want to ask your visitors to leave when you begin a feed; they will understand. At night, it's a good idea to have a small light to feed by, either in your bedroom or the nursery. Night feeds should be very quiet and restful, as you want your baby to settle quickly after the feed.

Feed Diary

A diary is something I have found very useful over the years, although it is not an essential part of feeding. Keeping a diary can help you to get to know your baby's feeding habits, and guide you in establishing a routine. Recording which breast you have fed from will remind you which side to begin feeding on next time. The headings below are my suggestions for a basic diary, but feel free to adapt them to your needs:

- *date*
- *time awake (or time woken for feed)*
- *time feed started*
- *which breast/s fed from if breastfeeding*
- *length of feed on each side if breastfeeding*
- *how much milk taken if bottle feeding*
- *length of time awake*
- *time settled for sleep.*

Bottle Feeding

If you have decided to bottle feed, or need to bottle feed when your baby is first born, you will need a good supporting bra. It's also important not to drink large quantities of fluid. Your breasts will feel uncomfortable for a few days, particularly around the third day when your milk is coming in. By the time your baby is a week old, if you have not put her to the breast to suckle your body will usually have absorbed the milk and your breasts will be returning to pre-pregnancy size.

How to Bottle Feed

To bottle feed your baby, hold him in the same basic position as you would for breastfeeding (see positioning, below), using a pillow to support him if you need to. Make sure you hold him close to you and spend time bonding with him and getting to know him in just the same way you would if breastfeeding. Warm the bottle and gather the things you need around you, and make sure you are warm and comfortable.

To start the feed, cuddle your baby close to you and put the teat to her mouth, and you will find that she will open her mouth wide. If she doesn't, tickle her mouth with the teat, and then put the narrow part of teat right into her mouth. She will begin to suck, and you will feel her pulling on the teat. As she sucks, don't push the teat further into her mouth or she can gag, but gently pull back on the bottle to encourage the suckling action. When you hold the bottle, the most important thing is to make sure there is always milk in the teat so that she isn't swallowing lots of air bubbles. Holding the bottle at an angle of about 45° to the ground should keep milk in the teat. You will definitely need to wind your baby during bottle feeding (see winding, page 64), as the milk tends to flow faster than from the breast and she may well gulp, especially at the beginning of a feed. To take the bottle out, gently push the teat towards your baby's cheek and ease it out of the side of her mouth.

Formula

Deciding which formula to use is often confusing. In my view, they are all equally good, so it's a matter of preference. Many mothers prefer to give organic formula nowadays. Formula should always be made up with boiling water. To make up a bottle, boil cold water in the kettle and let it stand for a few minutes. If you have a water softener installed in your house, make sure to use the drinking water supply to make up bottles, and it is recommended that you don't use mineral water.

Have your sterilized bottles ready, and put in the amount of boiled water that you require (measurements are on the side of the bottle in millilitres and fluid ounces). Add the formula, screw the top down, give the bottle a shake and leave to cool. If you need to cool it quickly, stand the bottle in a jug of cold or iced water. Once cool, bottles must be kept in the fridge and should be used within twenty-four hours. Once you have taken the top off and used the bottle for a feed, don't keep the milk until the next feed. You can keep boiled water in the sterilized bottles until you need to use it, but you will need to warm this up before you add the formula.

You can buy an electric bottle warmer, but these can breed microorganisms so make sure you clean them out. Alternatively you can warm the bottle in a jug of hot water, but be careful if you have toddlers or young children around. Make sure that you shake the bottle to disperse any 'hot spots', and test the milk by putting a little on your wrist before feeding. The milk should feel just lukewarm, and not at all hot. I usually recommend that you don't warm bottles in the microwave, as the heat can be very uneven.

How Much Formula Does My Baby Need?

When you first begin bottle feeding a newborn baby, you will find a good feeding guide for your baby's size on the side of the tin of formula. In each twenty-four-hour period, your baby should be having 150 ml per kg of body weight ($2^{1/2}$ to 3 fl oz of formula per lb of body weight). Divide this amount equally between six feeds a day, until he drops the night feed, when you will divide it between five feeds. Using this method, if your baby weighs 3.6 kg (8 lb), you should be giving him 500–600 ml (20–24 fl oz) of milk in twenty-four hours. So if your baby is having six feeds, each feed should be 80–100 ml (3–4 fl oz), and if your baby is having five feeds, each feed should be 100–120 ml (4–5 fl oz).

A good rough guide is to take your baby's weight in pounds (for example, 8 lb), divide this in half (4 lb) and convert this to ounces per feed (4 fl oz per feed). Don't worry if your baby takes the full amount at some feeds, and doesn't completely finish the bottle at others.

Giving Cooled Boiled Water

You can give 25 ml (1 fl oz or so) of cooled boiled water to your baby in the night, to help her begin to drop the night feed. You don't need to add any sugar or anything else to this. To prepare cooled boiled water, boil the kettle and fill a sterilized bottle. You can then keep this in the fridge until it is needed, and warm it up in a bottle warmer or saucepan before offering it to your baby. Boiled water can also be given to top up your baby's fluids if the weather is very hot, or if she is constipated.

Bottles and Teats

There are a number of different bottles on the market, and it's a good idea to decide which one suits you and your baby and then stick with it. You can buy wide-necked or narrower bottles, but be aware that you can't swap teats between these types of bottle. Some teats are harder than others, so if you are breastfeeding as well as bottle feeding you may want a softer latex teat, which is more like a nipple. For newborns, make sure you get a teat with a single hole in it, as this helps to encourage the sucking action. At about two months you will probably want to change to a two-hole teat to make sure he gets enough milk.

Sterilizing Bottles

You will need some way of sterilizing your bottles to keep them clean and free from infection. Sterilizers work by steaming bottles to kill any bacteria. I would recommend that you buy an electric rather than a microwave sterilizer, as they have a larger capacity and can be used anywhere. Alternatively you can use Milton liquid or tablets, which are dissolved in cold water. You will also need bottle brushes and a small brush to clean the teat; these are often sold in the pack with bottles. To wash the bottles and teats, put them in a bowl of hot soapy water, scrub with the brushes and rinse thoroughly in cold water. Always wash your bottles after feeding.

Sterilizers need to be kept clean and free from limescale, and if you have dirty marks on your bottles it may be because the sterilizer needs descaling. All sterilizers come with descaling tablets, but once these have run out you can use 10 g (0.4 oz) of citric acid powder (available in chemists) in 200 ml (8 fl oz) of water. Switch the sterilizer on and leave this solution in it for ten minutes without the lid on, switch off and leave for a further thirty minutes, and then rinse thoroughly. Before you sterilize any bottles, run the machine with 90 ml (3.6 fl oz) of plain water with the lid on and empty when finished. Alternatively you can make up a solution of 100 ml (4 fl oz) vinegar and 200 ml (8 fl oz) water and put this in the machine without switching on until the limescale has dissolved. Empty the unit, rinse and dry before using.

Bottle Feeding Twins

Ideally, you will want to bottle feed twins together. However, you will need your partner or someone helping you so that you can give a bottle to each twin at the same time. If you are feeding your twins on your own, feed and settle your most fractious twin first, even if you just give her a couple of ounces. Wind her and put her in her chair while you feed the other twin. You can then go back and finish the feed for the first one.

Using a Bottle When You are Breastfeeding

Introducing a Bottle with Expressed Breast Milk

In my view, it is always a good idea to introduce a bottle to your baby during the first month of life, using expressed breast milk. It can be very difficult to encourage a three to four-month-old baby to take a bottle if they have only breastfed before. It is likely that at some stage you will want others to be involved with feeding your baby, and introducing a bottle early on helps your baby to get used to this. When your baby is used to a bottle, the advantage is that your partner can help out with feeding, particularly with evening and night feeds if you are very tired.

To introduce a bottle to your breastfed baby, simply replace one feed with a bottle of expressed milk. It's a good idea not to do this at the first morning feed, when you have plenty of milk. A soft latex teat will help to reduce the contrast between breast and bottle for your baby.

Topping Up Breastfeeding with Formula

There may be times when your baby needs 'topping up' with a formula feed. This is quite acceptable, and doesn't mean that you're going to stop breastfeeding. Top-ups are often used if you have a very hungry baby and you don't have quite enough breast milk, for whatever reason. There is nothing worse for the whole family than a hungry, crying baby, so you don't need to feel guilty about topping up. As soon as you have given a top-up you will find that your baby is contented and you have peace in your house again.

If you are very busy, especially if you have other children, you will often find that you don't have enough milk to satisfy your baby at the evening feeds. Always breastfeed first, making quite sure that he has taken all the milk you have, and then top up with a bottle. He may only need about 25 ml (1 fl oz), so start with that and add another 25 ml if he is still hungry. I often top up breastfed babies at the 6.00 and/or 10.00 p.m. feeds with this amount of formula, as this takes longer to digest and can help them to feel full for longer.

Replacing the Night Feed with Formula

If you are very tired and want to have a good night's sleep, your partner can give a bottle of formula at the night feed. You will find that your breasts will be very full in the morning the first few times you do this. However, your milk supply will level out after a few days if you are giving a formula feed at night regularly. If you are trying to build up your milk supply, it is not a good idea to replace any feed with formula, as missing a feed gives your breasts the message to reduce milk production.

Weaning Your Older Baby onto a Bottle

You may want to give your baby some bottle feeds when she is older, particularly if you are going back to work. You may also want to reduce breastfeeding if you feel you have done it for long enough, or are feeling tired and drained. Some mothers want to do this when their baby is around three to four months of age; however, if your baby has never taken a bottle before, weaning her off the breast is going to be quite tricky. My heart does sink somewhat when a mother with an older breastfed baby asks me to help get her baby onto a bottle.

It is often easier if someone other than you introduces the bottle, as your baby will tend to smell your milk and refuse the bottle. If you can, try with a bottle of expressed breast milk in the first instance. Make sure that you have a couple of days free to persevere with bottle feeds. The milk needs to be warmed, as your baby will be used to warm breast milk. Use a nipple-shaped latex teat, as this will be softer for your baby's mouth. The teat should have a large hole so that the milk flows easily into his mouth, and you can enlarge the hole with a hot needle if you need to. Most importantly, make sure your baby is really hungry before you try the first bottle.

Hold your baby securely in your arms, sitting her up a little more than you would for breastfeeding. Put the teat into her mouth and hold it there reasonably firmly. You will probably find that she refuses the teat by turning her head away and spitting it out. Stay as calm as you can, and distract her by chatting and singing, or walking around the room to look at things. The most important thing at this stage is to persevere with offering the teat, as she will take it eventually. She may completely refuse the bottle at this first feed, in which case I'd advise that you don't offer the breast, and just try a bottle again a bit later on. At every feed for twenty-four hours, offer the bottle rather than the breast, and all of a sudden you will find that she sucks away hungrily and really enjoys herself. Both you and your baby will feel very pleased with yourselves at this moment.

Once your baby is happily taking expressed breast milk from a bottle, you can introduce formula either by itself, or mixed with breast milk if you wish. If you want to wean him completely off breast milk and onto formula feeds, you can gradually reduce the amount of breast milk mixed in. I have found this works well, but it really is easier all round if you have introduced a bottle in the early weeks.

In essence, I believe that whether you breastfeed or bottle feed your baby, feeding is a wonderful time of bonding and closeness. The experience of feeding is one of the most precious parts of parenthood, and will bring you great satisfaction.

CHAPTER 6

Establishing a Flexible Routine

Newborn and young babies' lives revolve around feeding and sleeping; this is really all they do in the first few days and weeks of life. In this chapter I hope to give you my suggestions for establishing a routine in feed and sleep times for babies from newborn to twelve months. This is not meant to lay down any hard and fast rules for you and your baby, but to give you some guidelines to help you and your family settle into a pattern.

Why is Routine Important?

There are a number of misconceptions about the idea of routine. Many parents feel that routine is a dirty word, and it is going to be too strict for them to apply. Parents often feel guilty that it is selfish to expect babies to fit in to their routine. They may also worry that there will be no time for bonding, affection and cuddles. My experience over the years has actually been the opposite.

My approach helps you to teach your baby structure in her day, and enables you to know when feed times are so that you can have structure in your day too. Feed times are an important time for you as parents, particularly to help you bond with your newborn. This continues to be a special time with your baby as she gets older, so give her lots of cuddles and affection when you feed her.

Demand feeding has been very popular over the past forty years and I believe that now the pendulum is swinging back. Many parents want to have some structure in their day rather than feeding their baby on and off all day. Over the years I have worked using a flexible feeding routine, and have found this very successful.

Why is there a need for routine in bringing up babies? Routine is the beginning of loving discipline, and babies and families thrive on it. When we think about it, we all have routine in our lives: we get up in the morning, we wash, dress, have breakfast, clean our teeth and so on, and mealtimes are normally at around the same time each day. There's no reason why this cannot apply to your baby's life too.

Routine is good for family life, especially if there are brothers and sisters. As parents, you know when feed time is going to be, so you can plan your day and have time in between feeds to rest or get on with other things. If you're going back to work and your baby is going into a day nursery or you're having a nanny, you will need routine. Babies in nurseries will normally need to conform to a routine, so your baby will feel happy and comfortable if this has already been established at home.

Why is Flexibility Important?

None of us want to be stuck with a rigid routine in our lives, so in bringing up our babies we also need to be flexible. Life often doesn't quite go to plan, particularly when you're busy with a new baby. If you're running late for whatever reason, it is perfectly all right to delay feed time slightly. Most importantly, some days you may find that everything goes wrong, and you get completely exhausted. I always say to parents, 'Don't worry – put it behind you and start again tomorrow.'

All babies are different. Small babies will need feeding more frequently in the early days. You may need to have top-up feeds if you have a hungry baby and he's ready before his feed is due (see Chapter 5). If you are starting a routine when your baby is older, it may take longer for him to adjust. Be patient and flexible and don't give up! In my experience, you can always encourage a fit, healthy baby into a routine.

Can I Use This Routine with Twins?

'With one baby, no one had suggested a routine with me. With twins and an eighteen-month-old, it was vital. Routine meant survival!'
Ruth Gray, mother of twins

If you have twins, a flexible routine is invaluable, otherwise you can soon find you're feeding around the clock. I have used the daily plans below with twins and they have worked very successfully. Generally, feed times will take a bit longer with twins and you may need to put one baby in her chair while you feed the other, if you are bottle feeding. If you are breastfeeding you can give feeds at the same time, with one twin on each breast in the 'rugby hold'. As far as possible, you need to wake, feed and settle your twins at the same time.

How Do I Apply Routine?

Over the years, I have used the following daily plans with many families, who have found them invaluable. I usually advise starting as soon as possible; however, if you are breastfeeding, during the first week or so it is important to feed on demand, little and often, to encourage milk supply (see Chapter 5).

The daily plans give you a guide for feed, bath and sleep times to help you establish a routine. The timings are what you're aiming for, and if it doesn't go quite to plan initially, don't worry, just persevere!

In each case, *the times given are when you should aim to start the feed,* or start putting your baby down to sleep.

Daily Plan, Nought to One Month (Four-Hourly Feeding)

Very young babies will often have a good shout when they are undressed, have their nappies changed, or are put in the bath. Don't worry if your baby does this – it is perfectly normal and he will soon start to enjoy these times with you. In the first two weeks or so, your baby may need to sleep again very soon after a feed.

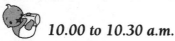 *10.00 to 10.30 a.m.*

- *Wake your baby up if she's not already awake.*
- *Top and tail (see Chapter 4).*
- *Dress baby in day clothes.*
- *Begin feed by 10.30 a.m.*
- *Feed and wind baby.*

- *Spend time cuddling and talking to baby.*
- *Change nappy if dirty.*

 ## 11.00 to 11.30 a.m.

- *Swaddle baby (see Chapter 7).*
- *Put baby in his cot or pram for a morning sleep.*
- *Baby can be taken out for a walk in the pram or buggy.*
- *Your baby will probably sleep until about 2.00 p.m.*

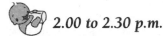 ## 2.00 to 2.30 p.m.

- *Wake baby if she's asleep.*
- *Begin feed by 2.30 p.m.*
- *Change baby's nappy either before or halfway through the feed, particularly if she's very sleepy, as this will help to wake her up and encourage her to feed again.*
- *Wind during nappy change.*
- *Finish feed.*
- *Spend time cuddling and talking to baby.*
- *Change nappy if you haven't changed it during feed.*

 ## 3.00 to 3.30 p.m.

- *Swaddle baby and tuck down in cot or pram.*
- *Baby can be taken out for a walk in pram or buggy.*
- *Baby will probably sleep until approximately 5.30 p.m.*

 ## Bathtime, 5.30 to 6.00 p.m.

Some people like to bath their babies before the 10.00 a.m. feed, but I prefer to bath babies at this time of the day, to establish the ongoing routine of evening bathtime. Giving a bath in the evening can help to relax your baby for sleep, and helps him to learn that bath and bedtime go together. If you haven't got the time or energy to bath your baby every day, this doesn't matter; top and tailing is fine.

If you are breastfeeding and your baby is upset and is obviously very hungry, feel free to give one breast to pacify before bathtime and continue feeding after the bath. I usually prefer to bath babies before feeding to avoid bathing on a full stomach, which can cause vomiting or posseting.

- *Bathtime (see Chapter 4 for details on bathing).*
- *Dress baby in night clothes.*
- *Use this time for cuddles and talking to your baby.*

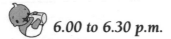 *6.00 to 6.30 p.m.*

- *Begin feed by 6.30 p.m.*
- *Spend this time quietly with your baby, as after this feed you will settle her for the evening in her cot.*
- *Wind baby.*
- *Only change nappy if dirty.*

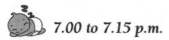 *7.00 to 7.15 p.m.*

This is the time of day when your baby will often be very unsettled. You will probably be told that this is colic. Usually it is not colic, but babies' wakeful time (see Chapter 8 on crying).

- *Ensure baby has had a good feed.*
- *Ensure baby has brought up all his wind.*
- *Swaddle and tuck baby into cot; this is the beginning of teaching him that this is night and not day.*
- *Your baby may sleep until approximately 10.00 p.m.*

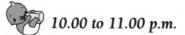 *10.00 to 11.00 p.m.*

Ensure that your baby has a really good feed at this time, as you want her to sleep for as long as possible. She may be sleepy during this feed, particularly if she hasn't slept well during the evening. It's very important to make sure she is winded well and has a clean nappy before you settle her for the night. I always aim to have my babies settled by midnight.

- *If baby is asleep, wake him by 11.00 p.m.*
- *Feed him.*
- *Spend time over this feed, sitting quietly with baby.*
- *Change nappy and wind halfway through feed.*
- *Finish feed.*
- *Swaddle and tuck into cot by 12.00 midnight.*

Night Feed

You do not need to wake your baby in the night for a feed, unless for medical reasons such as jaundice. Your baby will probably wake some time between 1.00 and 3.00 a.m., depending on when the last feed was. Give 50 ml (2 fl oz) of cooled boiled water (see Chapter 5) in a bottle instead of the night feed if she is just grumbling.

- *Feed when baby wakes.*
- *Change nappy only if dirty or he's sleepy during feed.*
- *Wind baby.*
- *Quietly tuck back into cot after feed.*
- *Baby will probably sleep for around another four hours.*

 ## 5.00 to 6.00 a.m.

- *Wake baby by 7.00 a.m. if she's not woken before then.*
- *Feed.*
- *Wind and change nappy.*
- *Make time for cuddles and talking to your baby.*
- *If baby is wakeful, she can be up for a little while.*

When your baby has been awake for up to one and a half hours, he needs to be tucked back in his cot to sleep again. Your baby will probably sleep until around 9.30 to 10.00 a.m., and then you start all over again. This is a complete twenty-four-hour routine for you and your baby. With four-hourly feeding, your baby will have six feeds a day if he wakes for a night feed.

Three-Hourly Feeding

Small babies under 3.2 kg (7 lb) in weight will often need to be on three-hourly feeds in the early days, progressing to four-hourly as they put on weight. Three-hourly feeding works in the same way but feed times will be different. With three-hourly feeding your baby will have eight feeds if she wakes for a night feed. You may find that after one feed she goes for four hours, and after the next she is back to three-hourly intervals. When she is ready, gently try to increase the feed time to four-hourly. Don't despair if it takes a little while to achieve this. Your baby will get there, depending on her weight and how she is feeding.

Daily Timings, Three-Hourly Feeding

Aim to begin the first feed between 9.00 and 10.00 a.m., with further feeds between the following times.

- *9.00 to 10.00 a.m. feed*
- *12.00 to 1.00 p.m. feed*
- *3.00 to 4.00 p.m. feed*
- *bath before the next feed*
- *6.00 to 7.00 p.m. feed*
- *9.00 to 10.00 p.m. feed*
- *night feed – don't wake to feed unless for medical reasons*
- *baby will probably wake to feed between 1.00 and 3.00 a.m.*
- *6.00 a.m. feed.*

Daily Plan, One to Two Months

This is virtually the same as four-hourly feeding for nought to one month, but your baby will have more wakeful times during the day. From four weeks onwards, your baby will be taking much more notice of his surroundings. After daytime feeds, he will be quite happy to sit in his chair or lie on your bed and have a look around. If you have a baby gym, he can lie under it and look at the mobiles.

9.45 to 10.00 a.m.

- *Wake baby (if baby is awake by 9.30 get her out of her cot).*
- *Top and tail.*
- *Nappy-free kick (take nappy off and let your baby have a good kick).*
- *Dress.*
- *Feed by 10.30.*
- *Wind baby.*
- *Time for cuddling and talking to baby.*
- *Wakeful time after feed for around twenty minutes.*

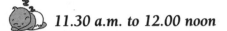 ### 11.30 a.m. to 12.00 noon

- *Swaddle and tuck baby into pram or cot.*
- *Baby can be taken out for a walk in pram or buggy.*
- *Your baby will probably sleep until around 2.00 p.m.*

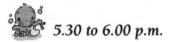 ### 2.00 to 2.30 p.m.

- *Wake and feed by 2.30 p.m.*
- *Change nappy before feed if baby is very sleepy, otherwise change halfway through feed.*
- *Wind baby.*
- *Wakeful time for around twenty minutes.*

You may find your baby sleeps for less time in the afternoon. If this is the case, it doesn't matter. As he gets older, he will have a long morning sleep and only nap in the afternoon.

5.30 to 6.00 p.m.

- *Nappy-free kick.*
- *Bathtime.*
- *Dress in nightclothes.*

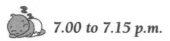 **6.00 to 6.30 p.m.**

- *Begin feed by 6.30 p.m.*
- *Quiet feed at this time, to settle for sleep.*
- *Wind baby.*

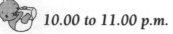 **7.00 to 7.15 p.m.**

This is bedtime, and in the second month of your baby's life you want to establish a regular pattern for bedtime which will last into childhood.

- *Ensure baby has had a good feed and is winded.*
- *Swaddle and tuck baby into cot.*
- *Your baby may be restless at this time; don't worry!*
- *Your baby may sleep until 10.00 p.m.*

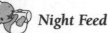 **10.00 to 11.00 p.m.**

- *If baby is asleep, wake her to feed by 11.00 p.m.*
- *Spend time over this feed, sitting quietly with baby.*
- *Change nappy and wind halfway through feed.*
- *Finish feed.*
- *Swaddle and tuck into cot by 12.00 midnight.*

Night Feed

Instead of the feed, 50–110 ml (2–4 fl oz) of cooled boiled water (see Chapter 5) can be given in a bottle in the middle of the night if your baby is just grumbling. Often this will help babies to settle again for another hour or so.

- *You do not need to wake your baby in the night for a feed (unless for medical reasons).*
- *Feed when baby wakes.*
- *Change nappy only if dirty.*

- *Wind baby.*
- *Tuck back into cot quietly to sleep for up to four hours.*

 ### 5.00 to 6.00 a.m.

- *Wake baby by 7.00 a.m. if he's not woken before then.*
- *Feed.*
- *Wind and change nappy.*
- *Make time for cuddles and talking to your baby.*
- *If baby is happy, he can be up for around one and a half hours from waking.*

How Do I Encourage My Baby to Sleep through the Night and Not Wake for a Night Feed?

From around six weeks your baby may be sleeping for a longer stretch during the night and may not wake until later in the night to be fed. If this happens, it's important not to wait for four hours until you feed her again. Feed and settle her again as soon as possible, and let her sleep until the next feed. Shortly she will begin to sleep until around 5.00 a.m., and then this feed can replace the first morning feed (7.00–7.30 a.m.). The table below outlines times for the morning feed if she wakes in the night.

Baby wakes for feed at	Feed again at
Before 3.00 a.m.	6.00–6.30 a.m
3.00 a.m.	7.00 a.m.
4.00 a.m.	7.00 a.m.
4.30 a.m.	7.30 a.m.
5.00 a.m.	No 7.30 feed
	Feed again at 9.45 to 10.00 a.m.
5.30 a.m.	No 7.30 feed
	Feed again at 10.00 a.m.
6.00 a.m.	No 7.30 feed
	Feed again at 10.00 a.m.

Daily Plan, Two to Three Months

At this stage, your baby will probably not need a night feed, so you will now have five feeds in a twenty-four-hour period. This routine is exactly the same as for babies of one to two months of age, but you will find that they are wakeful for longer periods during the day and taking more interest in what's going on around them.

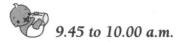 *9.45 to 10.00 a.m.*

- *Wake baby (if baby is awake by 9.30 get him up).*
- *Top and tail.*
- *Nappy-free kick*
- *Dress.*
- *Feed by 10.30.*
- *Wind baby.*
- *Time for cuddling and talking to baby.*
- *Wakeful time until he appears restless (up to two hours from waking).*

11.30 a.m. to 12.00 noon

Now that your baby is older, you do not need to swaddle her for sleep times during the day. She will probably be too big to swaddle by now anyway.

- *Tuck into pram or cot.*
- *Baby can be taken out for a walk in pram or buggy.*
- *Your baby will probably sleep until around 2.00 p.m.*

2.00 to 2.30 p.m.

- *Wake and feed by 2.30 p.m.*
- *Change nappy before feed or half-way through feed.*
- *Wind baby.*
- *Time for cuddles and chats.*
- *Wakeful time until he appears restless (up to two hours from waking).*

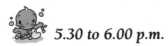 **3.30 to 4.00 p.m.**

This sleep time will just be a short afternoon nap, as your baby will probably not need to sleep for very long at this time of day.

- *Tuck into pram or buggy.*
- *Baby can be taken out for a walk.*

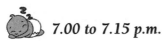 **5.30 to 6.00 p.m.**

- *Nappy-free kick.*
- *Bathtime.*
- *Dress in night clothes.*

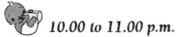 **6.00 to 6.30 p.m.**

- *Begin feed by 6.30 p.m.*
- *Quiet feed at this time, to settle for sleep.*
- *Wind baby.*

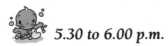 **7.00 to 7.15 p.m.**

By two to three months, your baby will probably be more settled in the evening and sleeping well, as she is spending more time awake during the day.

- *Ensure baby has had a good feed and is winded.*
- *Swaddle (if you can) and tuck baby into cot.*
- *Do not worry if your baby is still being restless at this time.*

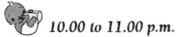 **10.00 to 11.00 p.m.**

- *If baby is asleep, wake him to feed by 11.00 p.m.*
- *Spend time over this feed, sitting quietly with baby.*
- *Change nappy and wind halfway through feed.*
- *Finish feed.*
- *Swaddle (if you can) and tuck into cot by 12.00 midnight.*

Night Feed

At this stage, your baby will probably be sleeping through the night, so the aim is to not have a night feed. If your baby is waking at around 4.00 to 4.30 every morning, and is obviously not waking from hunger, then try and encourage her to wait for her feed. She may grumble during this time; this is perfectly normal and she won't come to any harm with a wait of up to twenty minutes or so. If you continue to do this on a daily basis, you will find that very quickly she will be sleeping until 5.00 a.m., and you will have removed the night feed.

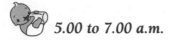 **5.00 to 7.00 a.m.**

- *Wake baby by 7.00 a.m. if he's not woken before then.*
- *Feed.*
- *Wind and change nappy.*
- *Make time for cuddles and talking to your baby.*
- *If baby is happy, he can be up for one and a half hours from waking time.*

Your baby should sleep until around 9.30 to 10.00 a.m., and then you start all over again. This is a complete twenty-four-hour routine for you and your baby.

What Happens if My Baby Wakes Early for a Feed?

Many parents wonder whether they should make their baby wait for her feed, or feed as soon as she wakes. Try not to pick your baby up as soon as she wakes, so that as she gets bigger she will learn to be happy in her cot or pram for a little while when awake. You may be busy or in the middle of doing something, and it won't hurt her to wait for a moment or two.

If your baby wakes early for a feed and is just grumbling, you could take him for a walk, as babies often settle themselves again with the movement of the pram. If you have got him tucked on his side, you could try turning him over onto his other side, as sometimes this will help to settle him again. If he is in a rocking cot, a few gentle rocks will often pacify him. If none of this works, and he is obviously very hungry, then feed him by all means. Normally you will then find he will be back on track for his next feed.

How Do I Apply My Baby's Routine When Travelling?

Many parents ask me how they should keep their baby's routine when travelling to a country with a different time zone. I usually advise that you keep your baby's bedtime in the local time zone. You may find that she needs top-up feeds during the day and little naps to keep her going, but try to make sure that she has her last feed by 10.00–11.00 p.m. local time and is then settled for sleep. Babies do get tired from travelling, so make sure she has plenty of naps and avoid overtiredness. If she does get completely out of sync, don't worry if you're only away for a few days, as you can get her back into her routine when she gets home. If you're away for longer, you can take a few days to adjust her routine to the new time zone.

Routine for Three to Six Months

By three to six months, your baby will probably be well and truly settled into a four-hourly feeding routine. The routine for three to six months stays much the same, the only difference being that you will drop another feed. This can either be the 10.00–11.00 p.m. feed or the 7.00 a.m. feed. You may prefer to drop the 10.00–11.00 p.m. feed if you need to get up for work or other commitments in the morning. I've found that most families prefer to drop this feed first. However, if you're a night owl you may want to drop the 7.00 a.m. feed and keep the 10.00–11.00 p.m. feed, and this is fine.

The other main difference in routine for three to six months is that you will be introducing solid food at some point. I usually advise that you give solids before your baby's milk feed, unless he is very hungry and needs pacifying with a short breast or bottle feed first. Try giving him just a few minutes on the breast or bottle, and then stop and give him his solid food. Use a bib, as you will find it really does protect his clothes, and solids can be a messy business. You can then continue his breast or bottle feed.

At three to six months you will notice a big change in your baby, as she starts to develop more social and physical skills. Your baby will be alert and wakeful, and will be happier for longer just playing and moving about. Plenty of playtime while she kicks and reaches for toys is good for her at this age, to exercise her muscles and help her physical development.

Daily Plan, Three to Six Months

Don't worry if your baby wakes a little early for his daytime feeds, as at this stage you can get him up and he will be very happy either on a play mat or sitting up in his chair or pram until feed time. He will probably be fascinated to watch you doing the cooking or household chores. He will love time just being with you and hearing you talking to him.

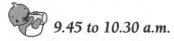 *9.45 to 10.30 a.m.*

- *Wake baby if you need to.*
- *Top and tail.*
- *Dress for the day.*
- *Begin feed/breakfast by 10.30.*
- *If giving solids start with food before breast milk or formula if possible (see Chapter 9).*
- *If not giving solids, feed.*
- *Change nappy only if dirty.*
- *Kick and play time – nappy-free if you prefer.*

11.30 a.m. to 12.00 noon

You may find now that your baby will sleep deeply for thirty to forty minutes and then stir and be unsettled for a few minutes. If you leave her and don't go and pick her up at this stage, she will usually re-settle and sleep well until about 2.00 p.m.

- *Tuck baby down for a sleep in pram or cot.*
- *Baby will probably sleep for about two hours.*

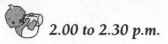 **2.00 to 2.30 p.m.**

- *If giving solid food, give some puréed vegetables for lunch followed by a breast or bottle feed.*
- *If not on solids, feed.*
- *Change nappy.*
- *Playtime or nappy-free kick.*

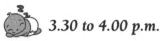 **3.30 to 4.00 p.m.**

You will probably find that your baby just has a short nap of about forty minutes in the afternoon, especially if he's had a good sleep in the morning.

- *Tuck into pram or buggy for a short sleep.*
- *When she wakes, take her for a walk or sit in her chair for a play.*

 **Teatime, 5.00 to 5.30 p.m.**

- *Give a drink of water or diluted fruit juice in a bottle or cup.*
- *If giving solid food, give a little bit of puréed fruit or mashed banana.*
- *Wakeful time to have a play or nappy-free kick before his bath.*

 Bathtime, 5.45 to 6.00 p.m.

- *Bath and dress in night clothes.*

6.00 to 6.30 p.m.

If you have not introduced teatime yet at 5.00 to 5.30 p.m., you can give your baby some buby rice before she has her milk feed.

- *Begin feed by 6.30.*
- *Story and quiet cuddle time to wind down for sleep.*

7.00 to 7.15 p.m.

Your baby should sleep well through the night now, because he has had more wakeful time during the day.

- *Tuck down for sleep.*
- *Turn out the lights.*
- *Your baby should be sleeping through until about 7.00 a.m.*

10.00 to 11.00 p.m.

- *If your baby is still having this last feed, wake her to feed by 11.00 p.m.*
- *Quiet feed (she may not wake fully during this feed).*
- *Change nappy.*
- *Tuck back down to sleep.*

6.00 to 7.00 a.m.

- *If baby is sleeping through, wake him by 7.30 a.m. (unless you want to drop the early morning feed).*
- *Feed.*
- *Change nappy.*
- *Tuck down into cot after he's been awake for about an hour.*

Dropping Feeds

Either the late feed (10.00–11.00 p.m.) or early morning feed (6.00–7.00 a.m.) can be dropped from around four months onwards. Some babies are nearer to six months before they are ready to drop a feed, so don't worry if your baby is not ready to go without one of these feeds until she's around six months.

Dropping the 10.00–11.00 p.m. feed
I usually find that once babies have started on solids, they are very sleepy at the 10.00–11.00 p.m. feed, and may not take all of this feed. If you notice that your baby is falling asleep and not finishing his 10.00–11.00 p.m. feed, this is very likely a sign that he is ready to drop this feed.

To find out if your baby is ready to drop the feed, don't wake her, and see how long she sleeps through for. You may find that she will sleep until around 5.00 a.m., and you can give her her early morning feed then, feeding again at about 10.00 a.m. You will find that she will soon sleep for longer, probably waking at about 6.00 a.m. for a few days, and eventually sleeping right through until about 7.00 a.m.

When you first drop the late feed, you may find that your baby sleeps well for the first few nights, and then begins to wake in the night to be fed. If he does this for several nights in a row, I suggest that you go back to giving him a late (10.00–11.00 p.m.) feed for about another week, and then try again when he's more ready to sleep through.

Dropping the 6.00–7.00 a.m. Feed
If you prefer to drop the early morning rather than the late night feed, continue to give your baby a good feed at 10.00–11.00 p.m. I usually find that babies having solids are able to sleep through until later in the morning if they still have this late feed. To see whether she's ready, don't wake her for the 7.00 a.m. feed, and see what time she wakes.

You may find that he wakes at about 8.00 a.m. but is quite happy playing and gurgling in his cot. He may well re-settle himself at this stage and may even surprise you by sleeping until around 10.00 a.m. It can take a few days to drop the early morning feed. Initially he may be wide awake by around 9.00 a.m., and this is fine as you can get him up, let him have a play and get him ready for the day. You may find you need to give the first feed at around 9.30, and he will gradually start sleeping for longer so that you can edge this feed towards 10.00 a.m.

If you find that your baby is waking and obviously hungry at about 8.00 a.m. every day, go back to giving her a 7.00 a.m. feed for another week and then try again.

Routine for Six to Nine Months

Between six and nine months, you will be gradually changing your baby's routine, as he will be eating more solid food. You will be moving on to what I call the 'three meals a day' plan, with breakfast, lunch and tea.

Most people continue giving breast or bottle milk at the 6.00–7.00 a.m. feed, but if your baby sleeps well you don't need to wake her for this feed. She can go straight on to breakfast at around 8.00–9.00 a.m. You may find that as your baby has more to eat at lunchtime, she will no longer be interested in milk and will only want water or diluted juice at this feed. It is a good idea to introduce a cup for drinks at this stage if you haven't already done so. She can drink from a cup at lunch and teatime too. You can drop the 10.00–11.00 p.m. feed if you haven't already, particularly if your baby is very sleepy and not taking a full feed at this stage.

You may find that on some days your baby is more interested in food, and doesn't want much milk. He may then have a day or two when he just wants milk, and this is perfectly normal. When he is teething or unwell, you will probably find that he doesn't want much food at all, so just give him plenty of milk and revert to solids as soon as he is ready.

Your baby will still have a good mid-morning sleep after breakfast; however, this will be earlier than in previous months. She will also probably still have a short nap in the afternoon. If she is having an afternoon nap, don't let her sleep for too long – ideally not longer than an hour – otherwise she may not settle easily at night.

Your baby is likely to really start moving around during this time. He will roll over, and may even start to crawl. If you have a playpen, this will be useful if you haven't already started using it. You will need to be aware of his movements, as he won't stay in one place when you put him down. Don't leave him unattended on the bed, and make sure he is strapped in when in his highchair, pram or buggy.

Daily Plan, Six to Nine Months

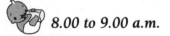 *8.00 to 9.00 a.m.*

- *Breakfast time.*
- *Baby can have cereal (with breast or formula milk).*
- *Other breakfast ideas are rusk, bread and butter or fruit.*
- *Give breast or bottle feed after breakfast.*
- *Time for play or going out after breakfast.*

10.30 to 11.00 a.m.

- Tuck baby down in cot or pram for a sleep.
- She may sleep until around 1.00 p.m.

 ## 12.30 to 1.30 p.m.

- Lunchtime.
- He can have some meat and vegetables and a dessert.
- Give breast or bottle feed if he wants it.
- You can give water or juice from a cup if he is not having milk.
- Playtime or out for a walk in the afternoon.

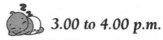 ## 3.00 to 4.00 p.m.

- Afternoon nap.
- Put baby in pram or buggy for a short sleep.

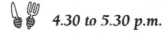 ## 4.30 to 5.30 p.m.

- Teatime.
- Baby can have a good meal of fruit or vegetables, becoming more substantial as she gets older, such as pasta or fish pie.
- She can have a drink of water or juice from a cup.

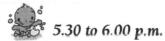 ## 5.30 to 6.00 p.m.

- Bathtime.
- Baby will really enjoy splashing and playing in his bath now.
- Make sure he is secure and safe in his bath.

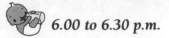 **6.00 to 6.30 p.m.**

- Breast or bottle feed.
- Quiet, winding-down time before bed.
- You could read a story or sing to baby.

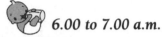 **7.00 to 7.30 p.m.**

- Tuck baby down in her cot.
- Settle her for the night.
- Your baby should now be sleeping through the night.

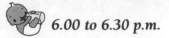 **6.00 to 7.00 a.m.**

- Give breast or bottle feed if baby is still needing it.
- By nine months, he may no longer need this feed.

If you prefer, your baby can have an early lunch around 11.30 to 12.00, and then have a longer sleep from around 12.30 to 2.30 in the afternoon. In this case, she would have just a short nap mid-morning at around 9.00 to 9.45 a.m. Some parents prefer to do this if they have school-age children as well as a baby.

Routine for Nine to Twelve Months

By the time your baby is around twelve months old, the aim is to have weaned him off the breast or bottle completely. However, it is completely your own decision when you fully wean your baby. When you have made up your mind that you want to stop breast or bottle feeding, I would advise that you do this gradually.

Many breastfeeding mothers find that once their baby is around a year old, they want to regain their body and are not keen on the idea of their toddler lifting their top up for a quick snack. If you are bottle feeding, it is important to wean your baby off the bottle before she can decide to go and get her own bottle out of the fridge.

You can begin to wean your baby by giving him his milk in a cup at breakfast, lunch and teatime. If you find he is still keen to have a breast or bottle feed at this stage, try going out for a walk to distract him. Initially, you may still be giving a breast or bottle feed at 6.00–7.00 a.m. and/or 6.00–6.30 p.m. I usually advise that you drop the morning feed first, continuing with the evening feed until your baby is around twelve months old. You may find that it is quite difficult to drop the evening feed initially, as this feed can be a comforting time when your baby is tired. Wean him off this feed gradually by giving him more milk at teatime in a cup so that he's full, and letting him suckle for a few minutes before he goes to bed. After a few days, you will find that he will settle without this feed.

Your baby will be well established in having three meals a day by this stage. She can sit up in her highchair for meals, and it is good for her to get used to eating with you at family mealtimes whenever possible. She will enjoy feeding herself, so let her have a spoon, even though you may need to guide her initially. This helps to lay a good foundation for enjoying food together as a family. If you are going out to a restaurant, you can take some food and drink for your baby if you're not sure whether there will be anything suitable on the menu.

Try not to overwhelm your baby with too much food on his tray, as he probably won't know what to eat first and you may have to throw a lot away. He can have finger food at this stage, and I usually advise that you give him small amounts at a time – he can always have a bit more if he's still hungry. You may find that this helps him to learn to finish his food well as he gets older. By the time your baby is twelve months old, I can assure you that you will have found that he can have full-fat cow's milk to drink instead of breast or formula milk.

By around twelve months, your baby will probably be having a long morning sleep which may last up to three hours. This will be her one daytime sleep, as she won't normally nap in the afternoon. Your baby may well be crawling, pulling herself up on the furniture, and beginning to walk. You may find that some days she is tired from all this exertion and needs a short nap in the afternoon.

Daily Plan, Nine to Twelve Months

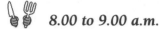 **8.00 to 9.00 a.m.**

- *Breakfast time.*
- *He can have cereal, porridge, toast, scrambled egg or similar.*
- *Give a drink of milk in a cup (cow's milk from twelve months).*
- *Playtime.*

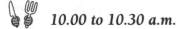 **10.00 to 10.30 a.m.**

- *Mid-morning snack.*
- *Give a small snack such as a rice cake, biscuit, rusk or fruit.*
- *She can have a drink of milk or juice in a cup.*

10.30 to 11.30 a.m.

- *Put baby down in his cot for a morning sleep.*
- *He will probably sleep for two to three hours.*

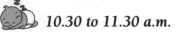 **12.30 to 1.30 p.m.**

- *Lunch time.*
- *Baby can have a good meal with a main course and dessert.*
- *Give a drink of water or juice from a cup.*
- *Playtime or a walk.*

4.30 to 5.30 p.m.

- *Teatime.*
- *Baby can have a substantial meal or plenty of finger food.*
- *Teatime ideas include sausage rolls, quiche, cheese and pieces of fruit or vegetables.*

- *Give your baby a good drink of milk from a cup if not giving a breast or bottle feed at 6.00–6.30 p.m.*

 ### 5.30 to 6.00 p.m.

- *Bathtime.*
- *Once your baby has teeth, help her to clean them.*
- *Your baby may be moving around and pulling herself up in the bath by now, so invest in a non-slip mat.*

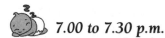 ### 7.00 to 7.30 p.m.

- *Winding-down time before bed.*
- *Read a story or sing songs.*
- *Tuck baby into his cot and settle for the night.*
- *Your baby will probably sleep through until breakfast time.*

By the time your baby is twelve months old, I hope you will have found that introducing a flexible routine means you have a happy and contented child who feeds and sleeps well. Having established this in the first twelve months, you will find that your child is better able to cope with the ups and downs of toddler life. Toddlers often gain a great sense of security from routine in an ever-changing world, for example using the same bowl for breakfast or having the same story at bedtime. As a family, you will ideally find that a good daily structure helps you to manage the inevitable tantrums that will come in the months ahead.

CHAPTER 7

Sleep

Many parents seem to have problems helping babies and young children to sleep nowadays. How often have you heard friends or family say that they are walking around the house at night to get their baby to sleep, or driving him round in the car to help him to settle? This usually stems from a lack of good advice for parents in training their newborns to sleep well. As parents, you are often advised to pick your baby up and feed him every time he cries, which can make it extremely difficult to get a good sleeping pattern going. It is a myth that having a baby will mean you don't get any sleep for the next three years. Babies need sleep in order to grow and develop, and they really can't have too much sleep; in fact, they thrive on it.

Babies who are taught to sleep early on will be happy and contented and will generally grow up to be good sleepers. Importantly, parents also need sleep! It is important to form good sleeping habits in the first few months of life to help your baby understand the difference between night and day. By six months of age, a baby with good sleep habits should regularly sleep through the night for at least twelve hours.

How Do You Know When Your Baby is Tired?

Understanding the Difference between Cries

Understanding your baby's cries is a learning process as you get to know her. It may take a while for you to understand different cries. Her cry for food will be different from her cry when ready for sleep. A cry for food will be much more desperate; in fact, she may be inconsolable and it will be difficult to quieten her. She may also suck her fingers or hand. The sleep cry will usually not be so desperate; she may well suck her fingers, but for comfort rather than hunger, as she will be longing to be put down for a sleep. Babies often make little noises in the night as they drift in and out of sleep, and this is quite normal.

Physical Signs of Tiredness

Sometimes older babies will begin to close their eyes and doze between periods of crying, and you then know that they are ready for sleep. When your baby is tired he may rub his eyes and yawn, and when he is put in his cot he will often turn his head away from you or from whatever is going on. At this point he just wants to switch off. He may also crawl up to the top of his cot to sleep.

How Long Has Your Baby Been Awake?

It's important to remember how long your baby has been awake, as this will help you to know when she's ready for sleep. Babies can get very overtired from being handled too much and passed around for people to hold, particularly in the first two months of life. Your baby can be overstimulated and then become very awake and aware of noises and things going on around her. At this point it can be difficult to get her to settle, so try to make sure she doesn't get to this stage. Bouncing or jumping your baby on your lap can also overstimulate her, so try not to do this before sleep. This doesn't mean that you, your friends and family can't have lots of cuddles and contact with your baby; just be aware that she may become overtired very quickly.

Colic

Many babies will be unsettled during the evening and this is often called colic. Normally it is not colic, just a time when they need to air their lungs and be wakeful (see Chapter 8). This is particularly true if they are sleeping well between feeds for the rest of the day. Babies often need to have one time of the day when they are wakeful, and unfortunately this is usually in the evening just as parents are sitting down to supper.

Length of Sleep

During the first forty-eight hours after birth, your baby will often have a long stretch of sleep. Don't worry, as this is perfectly normal. For the first two weeks of life, babies will often sleep most of the time, only waking or being woken to feed. Sometimes they may only be awake for an hour at any feed time. This is quite normal, particularly if your baby was born early. My daughters were born two weeks early and they both slept for the first fortnight of their lives, just waking for feeds. After two weeks they suddenly seemed to wake up and come to life.

Babies up to the age of around six months need about sixteen hours of sleep in every twenty-four hours. Some newborns will sleep even more than this. For the first few weeks, you should try to avoid your baby being awake for more than one and a half hours at feed time. Sometimes you will find one hour is enough.

As your baby gets older, he will gradually begin to sleep through the night, having a couple of hours of sleep in the morning and just a nap in the afternoon. As he starts to sleep through the night, he will usually go for one night without a feed, and then maybe want a night feed for the next couple of nights. Once he has slept through the night without a feed, you know he can do it in the future.

From about four to six months of age, babies will probably be sleeping through the night from about 7.00 p.m. until 6.00 a.m. or 7.00 a.m. Your baby should have a good morning sleep, and just nap sometimes in the afternoon. Try not to let this sleep be too near teatime (early evening feed) or he won't be ready for sleep at bedtime.

From six months to one year, her routine and sleeping will change, as she will be having three meals a day. She will be sleeping well through the night, from about 7.00 p.m. until 7.00 or 8.00 a.m. She will then either need to sleep in the late morning for a couple of hours, or have an early lunch (say 11.30 a.m.) and then have a two-hour sleep in the afternoon. Some days you will find she needs to have a little nap in the afternoon, depending on how good her nights are and on when she wakes in the morning. You may not find this necessary every day.

By twelve months old he will be having one good sleep a day and the odd afternoon nap, depending on what time he wakes in the morning. Each child is different, so this is just a guide: babies, like adults, vary in sleeping patterns and needs. I can't emphasize enough, however, that babies usually need to be taught when to sleep.

Where Should Your Baby Sleep at Night?

Many parents ask me whether they should have their baby in bed with them at night. I do not recommend that your baby sleeps in your bed, for two reasons: you might turn over in the night and smother her, and both parents and baby will sleep better separately. The Foundation for Study of Infant Death (FSID) advises that babies should not be in bed or on sofas or other places with sleeping parents, particularly if a parent smokes or has been drinking alcohol.

Before your baby is born, you and your partner need to discuss and agree where he is going to sleep. It is important to remember that you need time for each other, and sometimes space without your baby. For the first month of your baby's life, it is fine for him to be in his cot or Moses basket in your bedroom, and maybe you will want him to be with you for longer. It is quite acceptable for him to go into his own room from four weeks onwards, and even earlier if you prefer.

Where Should Your Baby Sleep During the Day?

I believe it's good for babies to sleep somewhere different during the day, to distinguish night-time from daytime. If you have a pram or buggy, by all means put your baby to sleep there during the day. I'm a great believer in taking babies for walks during the day if possible: babies love motion, whether in the pram or the car, and this can often help them to settle off to sleep. Young babies should not sleep for long periods in a bouncy chair or a car seat on a regular basis, as it is not good for their backs.

If you have a garden that is fenced and safe for you to leave your baby in, then she can have her daytime naps there, as the fresh air is good for her. If she is well wrapped up, it's fine for her to sleep outside even in the winter; however, it's useful to have a raincover for the pram. It's also a good idea to have an insect net for summer days.

Babies are much more comfortable when tucked down in their buggy or pram, and will have a deeper sleep, than lying in somebody's arms. However, don't worry if your baby falls asleep in your arms now and again. It's a good idea not to let this become a habit, though, as it can make it more difficult to teach him to settle himself. Never go to sleep with your baby on your lap on the sofa, as once you are asleep you will not be aware of your baby's movements.

In the first two weeks of life, your baby can sleep in the living room during the day, even if there is quite a bit of noise. As she gets older I would usually advise that she sleeps in another room, so that she will not be disturbed and you don't have to tiptoe around her.

There may be times when you want your baby to sleep in his cot in his own room during the day. In the early months you don't need to draw the curtains; however, from about four to five months of age I would advise that you draw the curtains, to establish this as a 'sleep time'.

Your Baby's Sleeping Environment

Monitors

Baby monitors are very popular now, but I am personally not very keen on them as they magnify every sound a baby makes and this tends to make parents jumpy. Having said that, they certainly have their uses, particularly if you live in a very large house or one with lots of stairs. Use a monitor with discretion.

Light Levels

Your baby certainly doesn't need a light on in her room at night, but it's a good idea to have a night-light to feed by. When you settle your baby down at about 7.00 p.m. it is a good idea to switch off the light, to help her learn that this is the beginning of night-time. Many parents wonder whether they should use blackout curtains. I usually advise against them, as your baby gets used to this level of darkness, and if you then go away to stay with friends or in a hotel where there are no blackout curtains, she will be unable to sleep.

Temperature

The most important point about temperature is not to overheat your baby. It is much better to have a cool room than one that is too hot. If your baby is sleeping in a nursery, it should be kept at around 16 to 18 °C. Feel the back of his neck if you are not sure; this should be just nicely warm, not hot and sweaty.

Babies lose heat very quickly when they go to sleep, so make sure she has enough covers on at night, depending on the time of year. In the winter months she may need a cardigan over her sleepsuit, a cotton shawl for swaddling and two cotton blankets. If the weather is very cold, I often put another blanket on after the last feed at night. In the summer, she may only need a vest on, and be swaddled in a cotton sheet with one blanket over her, again depending on the weather.

Swaddling

I always swaddle young babies. Your baby will sleep much better and feel more secure when wrapped up well. I like to use a cotton shawl or blanket, the size you would use for a Moses basket, around 70 by 90 cm (25 by 35 inches).

To swaddle your baby, fold the blanket in half to make a triangle. Lie your baby on his back in the middle of the triangle, with the point of the triangle under his feet, making sure that his head is just above the top of the blanket. To swaddle with both arms in, place his arms by his side, wrap one side of the triangle over his body and tuck it underneath. Then wrap the other side of the triangle over and tuck it underneath his body. You then have him nice and secure.

I sometimes swaddle babies with one or both hands near their mouths. To do this, lie your baby on her side, again in the middle of the triangle. Gently bring one or both hands up towards her mouth, and wrap the upper side of the triangle around her back and tuck under her tummy. Then bring the bottom side of the triangle up and over her back and tuck under her body. This will make her feel snug and secure, and lets her suck her fingers or hands if she wants to.

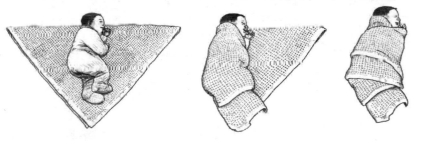

From six weeks onwards, particularly if your baby is big, you may not be able to swaddle her any more. Don't worry when this happens.

Positioning Your Baby for Sleep

This is a controversial issue at present, and over the last thirty-five years I have seen fashions come and go as to sleeping positions. Never put newborn babies on their tummy to sleep, as research into cot death has shown the risk is higher in this position. All the babies I have looked after, including my own, have slept on their sides, and in my view babies sleep better on their sides. This position is similar to the position in the womb, helping your baby to feel comfortable. If your baby is sick when asleep, the vomit can just dribble out of the side of his mouth. The FSID recommends that babies are best protected from cot death if they sleep on their backs until they are old enough to roll over easily and frequently, at around six months.

In the second month of life your baby will probably be turning from her side onto her back. If you decide to put your baby on her side to sleep, to help keep her there you can roll up a small cotton cot blanket and place it behind her back, and then tuck the sheet or blanket over her and the roll.

Your baby should be positioned fairly far down the mattress so that his feet are nearly touching the end of the cot. This is so that, if he wriggles, he will move up the cot, and not down under the covers. Make sure that the blankets are tucked under the mattress on both sides, and under his feet.

Helping Your Baby Settle to Sleep

It is very tempting to let your baby go to sleep on the breast, and very comforting for you too. However, it is not a good idea to do this regularly, as it can make it more difficult for her to settle herself. When your baby is very young, she will fall asleep on the breast naturally. To help her not get into a pattern of only being able to sleep on the breast, try to gently wake her up before you put her down to sleep after a feed. If you put your baby in the cot asleep straight from a feed, it is likely that she will wake again in ten minutes or so. If she is regularly put in the cot asleep after a feed, she

112

may cry out in the night every time she comes into a lighter sleep, wondering where you are.

If your baby is not able to settle away from the breast from an early age, this can form a habit that is very difficult to break by six to seven months of age. I have been called in to help numerous families who are having this sort of problem, where their baby has consistently settled himself on the breast from birth.

Put your baby down in her cot when she is awake from an early age, as again, this will help her to become used to settling herself. Sometimes she may take fifteen to twenty minutes to settle. Don't be afraid to let her have a good shout when you put her down after a feed, as she will usually settle herself. If she is sounding desperate after ten to fifteen minutes, pick her up and check that she hasn't got wind or a dirty nappy. If she is still hungry, it is fine to top her up with a short feed (see Chapter 5).

Comforters

I never use dummies or pacifiers, as I feel they are habit-forming. However, if you live in a place where your neighbours can hear your baby crying, it may be a good idea to use one in the very early days just to settle him if you are desperate. As soon as he is asleep it will drop out, and you don't need to put it back in again. After a couple of months, I advise that you take it away before it becomes a habit. Dummies can also be a source of infection if they are dropped on the ground or floor and put straight back into the mouth, and therefore must be sterilized.

A lot of babies and children suck their thumb or fingers, and I find this perfectly acceptable. You can teach a child not to do this when she is a little older by letting her do it at night and not in the day. Normally, she will grow out of it. I will often put a baby's thumb in her mouth when she is a few days old, and find that she soon takes to it and it becomes her natural way of settling and re-settling herself.

Many babies like to suck a muslin cloth from about three to four months of age. You can tie this to the bars of your baby's cot to ensure that he doesn't cover his face with it. If you have a rocking cot, many babies enjoy its motion, and just one or two rocks often helps them to settle. Musical mobiles or soft toys can also be used to comfort your baby.

Putting Your Baby Down to Sleep

The Golden Rules

When settling for a night sleep (about 7.00 p.m.):

- *Make sure your baby has a full tummy (see Chapter 5), does not have wind and has a clean nappy.*
- *Make sure your baby has been up for the right length of time.*
- *Swaddle your baby if she is still small enough.*
- *Put the nursery lights down low.*
- *Sit with her in a rocking chair and sing a lullaby, or just walk quietly around the room with her.*
- *Put her on your shoulder and pat her back gently.*
- *Put her on her side or back in her cot.*
- *Tuck blankets in around her body so that her head and neck are above the top of the blanket.*
- *Put a musical toy on if you like; this should play a gentle lullaby, which she will associate with bedtime.*
- *Say goodnight to her.*
- *Turn out the light and leave the room, leaving the door slightly open (this enables you to check on her during the evening without disturbing her).*

Hints and Tips

As your baby gets older, the winding-down process is important. Try to do the same things with him at night-time, so that he learns to recognize that this is bedtime. As he gets bigger, you can read a story to him and say prayers with him if this is something you wish to do. I did this with all my children from an early age, thanking God for a lovely day and asking to be kept safe at night.

Don't let well-meaning friends come and peer into the cot when your baby's trying to settle, as this can stir her into thinking it might be a good idea to get up. It is much better if you or your partner can do the settling process quietly, either on your own or together.

Don't interrupt your baby's natural ability to fall asleep – sudden loud noises such as doors banging, shouting or the telephone ringing can often wake him if he's dropping off to sleep. If you watch your baby fall asleep you will find that for the first ten minutes or so he may appear to be asleep, and then will stir and may even open his eyes again. This is the time when it's important that he is left alone and undisturbed.

Don't go to her immediately if she fusses, but give her a chance to settle herself. Sometimes babies will take twenty minutes or so to settle; this is quite normal, and you can just leave them to it. At night-time, don't get into the habit of putting your baby into the pram or car to get her to sleep, as this can be difficult to break once established.

Sleep Training Methods for Night-time

Sleep training is something you and your partner should discuss before your baby is born, so you have some idea of how you're going to tackle it. As I've already said, babies will normally need to be trained to sleep well. However, there are methods to help if you have a baby who is three months or older and is not sleeping well, or will only settle on the breast. I have used the following two methods of sleep training over the years, and these will help you to establish good sleeping patterns for your baby.

1. *Shout It Out (Cold Turkey)*

- *Follow the Golden Rules (as above) for putting your baby down to sleep.*
- *Put your baby in his cot and let him shout.*
- *He may shout for anything from thirty minutes to one hour the first couple of nights, so be prepared.*
- *He will then fall asleep.*
- *Check your baby, and you will find him sleeping soundly.*
- *If he wakes after thirty minutes or so, leave him again – he will not shout for so long this time.*
- *Repeat this process until feed time.*

This method works quickly, and in a few days your baby will be settling on her own and sleeping well. You need to be tough with this method, and resolve to see it through. It's important not to give in, or you will be back to square one. You and your partner need to be in complete agreement over this method. If you have close neighbours, you could tell them that you are doing some sleep training, or they may wonder what is going on!

2. *Controlled Crying*

If you can't bear to hear your baby crying for too long, this method may suit you better.

- *Follow the Golden Rules for putting your baby down, as above.*
- *Decide how long you are going to let him shout for before you go in for the first time (try to make it at least five minutes).*
- *Go in, but don't put the light on.*
- *Don't get him up.*
- *Stroke his tummy.*
- *Talk quietly to him, telling him it is 'night-nights' time, or saying 'shush'.*
- *Leave the room, leaving the door slightly open.*
- *Make sure there is not too much noise in the house.*
- *Leave him longer this time, say ten to fifteen minutes.*
- *If he is not settling, go in and repeat the process.*
- *Repeat this process until he sleeps, leaving longer intervals each time you go in.*
- *It can take up to two hours for him to settle fully.*

This is a very effective method of sleep training, but it usually takes longer than 'shouting it out'. It will take around one week to improve your baby's sleep pattern, depending on how long the bad sleeping habits have been going on. Sometimes babies who have been sleeping through the night will suddenly start waking in the night. If you have stopped the night feed, don't feed them at this stage; use the controlled crying method.

If you really cannot bear to hear your baby cry, you can try either sitting by the cot reading a book to yourself, or standing by the cot stroking her tummy and talking quietly to her until she falls asleep. The most important thing is not to get your baby up and out of the cot. These methods will take a long time to settle your baby, and it's important to be aware that they will establish a pattern in which your baby cannot sleep unless you are there in the room.

Sleep Training for Daytime Naps

Many parents have said to me that their baby won't nap in his cot during the day. If you want to establish a pattern where your baby can sleep in his room during the day, it is important to do this before he is three months old. Put your baby into his cot before he is very tired, close the curtains, put his musical toy on, stroke his tummy and tell him it is time to sleep. Leave the room, leaving the door slightly open. Don't pick him up if he cries, and go back to him after ten to fifteen minutes, stroke his tummy and tell him again that it is sleep time. Repeat this process until he has settled to sleep. You will find that this works within a few days, and he will then happily go into his cot for his daytime nap.

Why isn't My Baby Sleeping?

If your baby is not sleeping, there are a number of things you could check. She may be hungry, in which case you can give her a short top-up feed. To find out if she is hungry, pick her up. If she is bright and happy when you do this, she is probably just waking to play or out of habit rather than hunger. However, if she is putting her fists in her mouth and crying inconsolably, it is likely that she is hungry. At around four months old your baby may be waking in the night because she is hungry for solid food, and as soon as you have introduced this you will find that she will settle down to sleeping well at night.

Babies often wake from being too cold. Check his temperature by feeling his neck or tummy to make sure he's not too cold or hot, and adjust his clothing and blankets accordingly. If he is over three months old you can use a baby sleeping bag in colder weather.

She may be overtired; if so, just hold her close and cuddle her, rubbing her head and back gently until she settles. Sometimes another few minutes on the breast will help her to settle.

He may have wind, so put him on your shoulder and walk around with him, rubbing his back for a few moments. When he is teething, from around four months, his cheeks may be red and he will be dribbling. He may also have a sore bottom and loose stools. This is the time to use a teething gel or granules and give infant paracetamol if needed. Finally, he may be unwell, in which case you should seek medical advice from your doctor.

In all difficult times regarding sleep, try to stay calm. This is easier said than done when you are tired. Babies pick up on anxiety, and the calmer you and your voice are, the better. A calm soothing voice will be better for your baby.

Summary

Sleep training ideally begins in the early days and weeks, but it is never too late to start. It is just more difficult, and can take longer for an older baby. If your baby wakes in the night, always remember that night-time is a quiet time, not a playtime. Establishing a bedtime routine as early as possible is important, as babies in this pattern tend to grow into toddlers who are happy to be in bed by around 7.00 p.m. and generally sleep well through the night.

CHAPTER 8

Crying

I find one of the things new parents worry about most is their baby crying, and how they should cope with it. Anxiety about your baby crying is natural; however, babies need to cry as they can't talk, and crying is an important part of their expression and development. A good cry doesn't harm your baby, and in the early days of life it can help to expand the lungs and is a sign of healthy development. In fact, if our babies didn't cry we would worry.

Babies have hugely different personalities, and some cry more than others. If your baby has cried a lot in the first few weeks of life, by the time she reaches six weeks she will cry considerably less. It may seem to you that your baby cries a lot more than other people's, but don't worry, as all babies can be encouraged to cry less. My approach involves not picking her up each time she cries, which teaches her to settle herself. This can initially seem quite counter-intuitive, as we all have an inbuilt reaction to pick up a baby as soon as we hear it crying. As you get to know your baby, you will learn a huge amount about the reasons she cries and how to comfort her.

Reasons for Crying

There are a number of reasons why babies may cry:

- *hunger*
- *tiredness*
- *pain or discomfort*
- *temperature (too hot or cold)*
- *needing attention/contact*
- *unfamiliar events (for babies older than three months).*

If your baby is well and healthy and yet cries on and off during the day and night, he is probably crying because he is hungry. You will notice that he wakes frequently between feeds and may only settle for a little time after being fed, and at other times he may not settle at all. He may also suck his fists and be quite agitated. You may find that he sleeps well after one particular feed; however, this may be due to being overtired.

Normally, a baby who cries with hunger is not getting enough to eat, and this can be easily rectified. If you are breastfeeding, you can add more feeds during the day. You can also increase the length of each feed, making sure that your baby reaches the hindmilk, which fills her up. If you have done all of this and your baby still seems hungry, I would suggest that you top her up with 25 ml (an ounce or so) of formula suitable for her age at one or two feeds during the day. Try this for a couple of days, and it should satisfy her hunger. I usually do not recommend that you top up with formula at more than two feeds a day, as you may find that your milk supply lessens. For hungry bottle fed babies, you can increase the feed by 25 ml (1 fl oz) at each feed.

When your baby is full and satisfied, you will find that the constant crying stops. Your baby will be happy and contented, and will probably need to be woken for a feed rather than waking by himself. Time and time again, I have found that hunger is the primary cause of constant crying, and once this need is met both baby and parents are much happier.

Another sign of hunger is failing to gain weight, which your health visitor will alert you to. Babies should gain, on average, 170–230 g (6–8 oz) a week until the age of three months. If your baby is vomiting or has a reflux problem, he may be unable to keep enough of his feed down to gain weight, and will often be hungry and in pain. If this is the case, you need to see your doctor.

Crying due to Tiredness

Your young baby should be having around sixteen to eighteen hours of sleep per day. Some babies need more than others, and you are fortunate if yours needs more! Some will survive on much less, but it is important that you don't let your baby get overtired. If she has been up for a while, and you know that she has had a good feed and been winded, it is very likely that she is crying because she wants to be tucked down to sleep. A tired cry will not normally sound as desperate as a hungry cry, and your baby will be showing all the physical signs of tiredness (see Chapter 7).

Preventing overtiredness is crucial to help you avoid a situation where your baby becomes increasingly fretful and difficult. I have found that many new parents don't put their baby down to sleep soon enough when he is crying, because they feel a need to stop him crying completely before tucking him down.

If your baby is overtired and crying, swaddle her, cuddle her close and then put her into her cot and tuck her securely in. You may find that she cries on and off for another ten minutes or so. If possible, try to leave her to settle herself. Normally during this time she will have a good shout at the beginning, which will gradually decrease until she stops and goes to sleep.

Crying due to Pain or Discomfort

Minor illnesses such as colds, ear and chest infections are quite unusual in young babies. However, in my experience babies with older siblings tend to be more susceptible to these illnesses in the early months of life. Ear infections will cause discomfort to your baby when sucking, and he will probably cry when feeding, and on and off during the day. Chest infections and colds will make it difficult for him to feed, and he will often cry because of this. If your baby has an ear or chest infection he will usually have a raised temperature, and you will need to see your doctor.

If your baby has gastroenteritis (vomiting and diarrhoea), this can cause crying due to pain and discomfort. You need to see a doctor as soon as possible, as your baby can dehydrate very quickly.

Babies will cry when they are teething. From around four months, your baby will show signs of teething including dribbling, red cheeks, sucking her fingers or fist, and crying more than usual. Teething can also cause a sore bottom and loose stools, which may make your baby uncomfortable. She may also wake up crying in the night because of pain in her gums. Infant paracetamol will soothe the pain and help her to sleep. You can also use teething granules, gel or teething rings. Teething pain comes and goes, and I've often found that cutting the tooth doesn't seem to cause as much pain as the development of the tooth in the gum.

Another cause of crying is wind or colic. Some babies suffer more from wind than others, and it is important to make sure that your baby has brought up all his wind during and after a feed. Your baby may cry during a feed and pull away from the breast or bottle because he has wind. If he does this, don't worry about stopping the feed and winding him (see Chapter 5 for winding techniques). Your baby may also bring his knees up, tense his body and cry in pain after a feed. If he shows these signs, he definitely needs winding. If you put your baby to sleep after a feed, and after about fifteen to twenty minutes he wakes up screaming, it could well be that he needs to be winded.

If your baby is uncomfortable, she may well cry to let you know. The best position for young babies to sleep in is to be flat, and if she has been in a car seat or chair for a while, her back may hurt and she will cry. Moving your baby and laying her flat will often help her to be comfortable and stop her crying. Your baby will also cry out suddenly if her head is not supported and flops back. Make sure when lifting and holding her that her head is securely supported.

Crying due to Changes in Temperature

Your baby will wake and cry in the night if he is too cold, even if he is not hungry. Make sure he has enough covers on and is tucked in well to prevent him kicking the covers off. Once your baby starts moving around in the night, it is easier for him to wake from the cold; a baby sleeping bag can help here. When out and about in the buggy or pram, make sure he has the right clothing and enough covers to keep him warm.

Your baby can also cry due to overheating. If this happens, her neck will be very hot and her face will be red. It is very important to cool her down by removing some of the covers, or clothes if it is very warm. Check the temperature of the room (ideally 16 to 18 °C). In a pram or buggy, your baby can easily get too hot if you have the raincover on and the sun comes out, or you go into a warm shop. Remember to take the cover off and let her have some air.

Crying for Attention or Contact

Newborn babies are much more likely to cry from physical need than specifically to get your attention. However, babies do love physical contact and cuddles, and if you have checked that his physical needs are met and he is still crying, perhaps he just needs some close contact with you.

As your baby gets older and is spending longer awake in the daytime, she may cry simply to get your attention, or even cry if you leave the room. This often happens from about three months onwards, as your baby does not yet fully understand that when you leave her, you have not disappeared and you will return. To deal with this, you can continue to chat to her and reassure her that you are coming back. Often, rushing to pick your baby up in this situation can actually increase her anxiety about being left. Talking reassuringly will help your baby to become used to settling herself and being happy in her own company. However, if she is obviously very distressed, pick her up and give her lots of cuddles to comfort her.

To help your baby get used to you coming and going, you can leave him in his chair or playpen and let him watch what you are doing. A few familiar toys around him will help him to feel secure, and provide a useful distraction.

Unfamiliar Events

From around three months of age, you will notice that your baby is becoming aware of her surroundings and of new people. She may well cry when you take her somewhere new, or introduce her to somebody she has not met before. Her bottom lip may tremble and she may look very miserable, and she will then usually let out a huge wail. This can be rather off-putting for the new friend! Often, your baby will just need a chance to look at the new person while you cuddle her and talk to her reassuringly.

When taking your baby somewhere new, you can help him to feel secure by taking his favourite cuddly animal or special toy. If you are staying away overnight, make sure he has his own blankets from home. He is likely to cry and perhaps look a bit frightened and unsure, so again it's important to reassure him and give him lots of cuddles.

Also from around three months, sudden noises such as loud bangs or shouting can give your baby quite a shock. She is likely to cry out and look startled, but if you talk calmly to her and cuddle her this will often soothe her quickly.

From around six months, when your baby is becoming mobile, you will find that he will cry in frustration when he can't move around as much as he would like. A change of scenery and some different toys can help to ease this frustration. Once your baby is moving around more easily, he will have bumps, knocks and falls that will cause him to cry. The most important thing at this stage is to avoid being over-anxious. If you can go calmly to your baby, say something like 'Oh dear, you've had a bump' and rub it better, this will help him to feel positive and confident about trying again. As with any unfamiliar events, a calm approach from you will help decrease your baby's anxiety.

Dealing with Crying at Specific 'Problem Times' of the Day

'Rachel was the first maternity nurse to teach me the value of letting a baby cry, and how that can be invaluable in setting up a routine.'
   Maymie White, fourth baby

Waking Early Before a Lunchtime Feed

Sometimes your baby will wake and cry before her lunchtime feed is due. You may not want to feed her early, to avoid upsetting her daily routine. If possible take her for a walk in the pram to settle her, rock her in her cot, or put her in her bouncy chair. You can often ease her crying for a while by holding her on your lap and giving her a cuddle. If, having tried all of this, she is obviously wailing with hunger, then by all means feed her.

Crying between 5.00 and 7.00 p.m.

Between the ages of one and two months, your baby will probably be sleeping less during the afternoon, and will be fretful and awake from around 5.00 p.m. onwards. Many parents ask me what they should do with their babies if they are crying and unsettled in the early evening before bath and feed time.

To help with this fractious time of the day, I often advise parents to sit their baby up in his chair for a little while to have a look around. This often provides enough distraction to stop him crying. You could take him for a walk or hold him on your lap, and older siblings can also help to amuse him. If this doesn't work, give him 25–50 ml (a couple of ounces) of cooled boiled water or baby juice in a bottle. About twenty minutes before bathtime, you could try having some nappy-free play time, which your baby will enjoy and look forward to as part of his bedtime routine.

Evening Crying

For some unknown reason, many babies from around two weeks to three months of age seem to have their most wakeful and fretful time in the evening. The only consolation for you is that the majority of your friends with babies will have experienced the same thing. All of my own children were unsettled in the evening from the age of two weeks. I often refer to this time as your baby 'having a good shout', and this has helped many parents I've worked with to differentiate between crying due to unmet needs, and 'shouting' during a normal period of wakefulness.

You may find that your baby sleeps for an hour or so after the 6.00 p.m. feed, and then wakes and has a good shout for no apparent cause. In some cases, your baby will not settle well, and will shout on and off all evening. For new parents, this can be very difficult to cope with, and extremely wearing. This is the time of day when you want to sit down and have a meal, and if you have other children it may be their bedtime. If your baby sleeps well and is settled for the rest of the day, evening crying is very likely simply her natural wakeful time, and as a family you need to decide how you are going to deal with this in order to preserve your own evening routine and your sanity.

If your baby has slept for an hour and then woken up, leave him to shout for about ten minutes to see if he will settle himself. If he doesn't, go into his room quietly and pick him up and put him on your shoulder, rubbing his back to check for wind. You will probably find that he stops crying immediately and looks around as if to say 'This is rather nice!' Once he is quietened, it's important to swaddle him and tuck him back into his cot fairly quickly. You can put him onto his other side if he is still sleeping on his side. I advise that you leave the room and allow him to settle himself again. Your baby may not settle properly during this period, but you will find he has short, light naps and is ready to be fed again at around 10.00 p.m. If you can leave your baby to have a bit of a shout on and off, he won't come to any harm. You will find that he settles extremely well after the next feed, and often sleeps for a good long stretch.

Many of the families I've worked with have initially found it difficult to leave their baby shouting, which is understandable. If you are finding it hard to use the above method, pick your baby up and carry her around with you or hold her on your lap until she settles and can be tucked down again. It might be better for your partner to do this, as if you are breastfeeding, your baby will smell your milk and cry to be fed even though she is not hungry. Once awake, your baby is likely to put her fists in her mouth and appear hungry, but this is often because she is unsettled. If you walk your baby around for a long time during the evening, she can become very overtired and may not take enough milk at the next feed. This can unfortunately lead to more wakeful nights with a hungry baby.

Crying during the Night

Some babies cry out in sleep without waking, and will re-settle themselves within five to ten minutes. I always advise parents not to get up immediately on hearing their baby crying at night, particularly if weaning him off the night feed (see Chapter 6). If your baby is still having a night feed and wakes crying, you don't need to get up immediately as he may settle for another half an hour or so, and will wake again when he is hungry.

If you find that your baby cries every couple of hours or so at night, it could be that she has an insatiable appetite. To help with this, you can offer more feeds during the day and some cooled boiled water (see Chapter 5) at night. Rather than offering her more feeds during the night, you can try turning her over onto her other side. Very often babies will settle themselves when turned over.

Crying and Family Life

The Effect of Crying on Parents

All babies cry, and the effect of crying on family life can be extremely wearing. Although some babies have an almost peaceful cry, others are real 'screamers' and their high-pitched, loud cry can feel very demanding. I often say to parents of a screamer that it's helpful to remember that your baby is not intending to wear you down and upset you. You may well have friends with babies who hardly cry at all, but try not to let this get to you. Your baby's crying is much more down to his personality and individual make-up than your parenting skills.

Many parents feel tremendous guilt about how they deal with crying. I feel it's very important to know that your baby will not remember or hold it against you if you do not pick her up every time she cries. With a first baby, you tend to be very anxious about crying, but you will often find with subsequent babies that you are more relaxed about crying as you have a busier home and other children to attend to.

If you do have a baby who cries a lot, for whatever reason, it is important to have strategies for coping. First, sharing the load with your partner, a relative or friend will enable you to have time out for yourself. This can be very valuable in helping you to put things in perspective. If your partner can take over responsibility for the baby for an hour or so, a long soak in the bath with a good book is a great remedy. Babies pick up their parents' anxiety, so if you have had some time to relax and become calm again, this will help you to settle and comfort him more effectively. Ask a friend or relative to babysit so that you and your partner can go out and have some time together.

Dealing with a crying baby can be incredibly stressful, and it is important to acknowledge this. Don't be afraid to talk to health professionals, friends or relatives if you are getting to the end of your tether. Once you are able to talk about it, you will find that this can ease the burden of feeling you are coping alone. If you get to the stage where you feel you are losing control, and may even harm your baby, it is most important that you go into another room immediately, and get help by contacting a friend or a group such as the UK organisation Cry-Sis (see Further Resources).

The Effect of Crying on Family Life

If you have other children, you may be concerned that your baby's crying will disturb them at night. If your child wakes when the baby cries, go to her and reassure her that everything is all right and it's time to go back to sleep, as you are dealing with the baby. However, you will be surprised how quickly your child will learn to sleep through when the baby cries.

During the daytime, as long as your baby is fed and clean and comfortable, it is important that you make time to spend with your other children – even if the baby is having a good shout. Toddlers particularly will not understand why a new baby is crying, and will often want your attention when you're trying to deal with the baby. Try not to exclude your toddler, and let him sit with you while you comfort your baby. If your baby is crying during the day, you can help older children feel special by letting them chat to him or show him their toys to help console him.

If you have neighbours who are disturbed by your baby's crying at night, as a very last resort you could use a dummy or pacifier. My advice would be to use it for as short a period as possible, until your baby is settling herself again.

Conclusion

My aim in this chapter has been to alleviate parents' fears about their baby crying. I hope you will feel you have been provided with some tools to understand why your baby cries, and how to cope with it when it happens.

CHAPTER 9

Introducing Solid Food

Many parents worry about when and how they should begin to give their baby solid food. This chapter aims to give advice on starting solid food, what foods you can give at different stages, and how to progress to three solid meals a day. There are two main reasons for starting solids: to satisfy your baby's increasing appetite, and to introduce him to the pleasure of new tastes and textures. Food is an enjoyable and social part of life, so don't be afraid of this new experience for your baby.

When to Start Giving Solids

Current advice is that you should not start solids before your baby is four to six months old. However, I personally feel that weight and signs of hunger are a better indicator than age of readiness for solid food. If your baby is large at birth, for example, 4–4.5 kg (9–10 lb), you may find she is ready for solids before four months of age. It's important to stress, however, that when you begin solids, they are not a replacement for milk. You should continue to give all the normal milk feeds, and add solids as something extra.

Signs of Readiness for Solid Food

Once your baby is 5.5–6.5 kg in weight (12–14 lb), you may find that he begins to wake in the night for a feed, having been sleeping through before. You may also find that he doesn't settle well between feeds, and seems to need more frequent feeds. If bottle fed, your baby will take a full bottle of 175 ml (7 fl oz) at each feed, and will still seem hungry. If your baby is showing these signs, he may well be hungry for more than just milk, and you can give solids a try.

Equipment for Solid Feeding

You will need some soft-tipped plastic spoons to feed your baby, as these are more comfortable in her mouth than metal ones. If you don't have plastic bowls, you can use the lid of a feeding bottle to mix up a small amount of baby rice or purée. If you are going to make your own purées and freeze them, you will need some ice cube trays for small portions, and plastic storage containers for larger portions. Your baby will probably get very messy when she eats solid food, so you will need plenty of bibs, and may want a muslin for your own lap when feeding her. It's also a good idea to have a plastic mat to go under the highchair, particularly as she gets older and begins to feed herself.

It is easiest to feed your baby when he is sitting up in his chair, but you can feed him on your lap, supporting him with your free arm around his back. When your baby is very young, he can be fed sitting in a bouncy chair, and from around six months he can probably go into a highchair if he is big enough.

Feeding Equipment

You will need:

- *plastic weaning spoons*
- *plastic bowls or bottle-lids for small amounts of food*
- *ice cube trays for freezing purées*
- *plastic storage containers for food*
- *bibs*
- *bouncy chair for the first few months*
- *highchair later*
- *plastic mat to protect floor under feeding chair (optional).*

Hygiene When Preparing Food

When preparing food for your baby, it is important to remember to wash your hands, and keep the food preparation area clean. If you want to, you can use an anti-bacterial spray or wipes to clean chopping boards, work surfaces, and your baby's highchair.

When you first begin giving your baby solid food, plastic spoons and bowls will need to be sterilized before use. Once your baby is six months old, you can use the dishwasher if you have one, or wash bowls and spoons well by hand.

Introducing First Solids

The best solid food to start with as a 'first try' is baby rice, which you can buy in a packet or make your own by cooking rice in unsalted water and puréeing it. If using packet baby rice, mix a teaspoon of rice with warm breast milk or formula, with no added sugar or salt. Mix the milk and rice together to a loose dropping consistency, and make sure it is lukewarm. If using cooked puréed rice, add warm breast or formula milk to the same consistency.

I usually advise that you give the first try of baby rice at the 10.00 a.m. feed, ideally before your baby has had any milk. However, if she's very hungry, give her a small amount of milk first, and then take her off the breast or bottle and put her in her chair to try a few mouthfuls of rice.

Make sure your baby has a bib on, as he will get messy. Put a little bit of rice on a plastic weaning spoon and put it in his mouth, resting the spoon on his tongue for a few seconds. He will suck the rice off the spoon, and may make a face at you and spit it out. If this happens, scoop up the rice and try it again. You will be quite surprised how quickly he begins to enjoy this new experience. In the first few days, he will probably want up to about five teaspoonfuls. You will know when he's had enough, as he will start to turn his head away and push the food out with his tongue.

After your baby has had as much rice as she wants, give her a full breast or bottle feed. If your baby really doesn't seem to be enjoying solid food, maybe she isn't ready, so take some time off and try again in another week or so.

Introducing Purées

Once your baby is enjoying rice and milk, you can add some well-puréed fruit or vegetables. To make a purée, peel the fruit or vegetables, steam or boil until soft (with no added sugar or salt) and drain the water off. Once the fruit or vegetables are well cooked, purée them in a blender or push through a sieve. The UK company Lakeland Plastics makes a very good baby steamer, which cooks and purées food (see Further Resources).

Below is a rough guide to introducing some purées into your baby's first solid feeds. Don't worry if it takes longer than three weeks for your baby to get used to fruit and vegetables with his baby rice. Some babies are hungry and take to solid food very quickly, and others take longer. If your baby does not seem hungry enough for three solid feeds a day by the third or fourth week, just keep him on two solid feeds for a bit longer.

Week 1

In the first week of giving solid foods, give your baby some baby rice once a day at the 10.00 a.m. feed, giving only breast milk or formula at the other feeds. Towards the end of this week, you can try mixing some puréed fruit (apple or pear) into the baby rice. You will probably find that she loves this, especially pear, as it's very sweet. The sugar in fruit is fine for babies as it is natural and unprocessed.

Week 2

In the second week, give some solid food twice a day, at the 10.00 a.m. and 6.00 p.m. feeds. It's a good idea to give baby rice at the evening feed, as this will help your baby to feel full for longer, especially if you are at the stage of dropping the 10.00 p.m. feed. Continue to give him his full milk feed alongside the solid food. Alternatively, he can have his second feed of solids at around 4.30–5.00 p.m., with a drink of water or juice. Then he can just have his breast or bottle feed at around 6.00 p.m.

Your baby can have fruit purée without rice at the morning feed, although she may need a little rice to take the acidity away. I find mashed banana can be rather indigestible if you offer it before she has got used to fruits and vegetables in her diet. Some babies love it and others don't, so if your baby gags on it leave it out of her diet for a few days and then try again.

Week 3 Onwards

From the third or fourth week on, you can give your baby solids three times a day, adding a solid feed at lunchtime, around 2.00 p.m.

You can now give him puréed vegetables such as sweet potato, carrot or parsnip. If you prefer to give your baby vegetable purées before you introduce fruit purées, to get him used to savoury flavours, this is fine. Again, give him a full milk feed alongside his solid food. You may find that the more he has at lunchtime, the less milk he will take at this feed. Don't worry about this, as it's quite normal.

Foods Suitable for Purées

You may not have thought about making your own baby food, but it is very easy and economical. Even if you don't normally do a lot of cooking, I would encourage you to have a go, as you will probably find it very satisfying. Making baby food at home means that you know exactly what ingredients have gone in, and you can give your baby a huge variety.

Babies generally seem to love fruit purées. The main thing to remember is not to start with fruits that are very sharp, such as cooking apples, blackcurrants, gooseberries and rhubarb. The fruits I usually cook and purée are apples, pears and apricots. You can also give purées of avocado, banana and mango, which do not need cooking.

Babies seem to like vegetables with quite a sweet taste at first, such as carrot, sweet potato, butternut squash, parsnip, swede and courgette. Later on, you can try giving purées of green vegetables such as broccoli, peas, green beans and spinach. These vegetables can be mixed with a little carrot or sweet potato, especially if your baby is not very keen on them. Ordinary potato makes a good base for mixing with other vegetables or some mild cheese.

It's good to give your baby a wide variety of different tastes in purées. If you try a new fruit or vegetable one day and she spits it out, don't worry that she'll never eat it. You may find that if you try it again in a few days time, she will eat it heartily. Feel free to make mixtures of different purées, as this can help her to enjoy lots of variety.

How to Freeze and Store Home-Made Baby Food

When you've made a batch of puréed fruit or vegetables, the best way to freeze it is in an ice cube tray. Before tipping in the purée, make sure the ice cube tray is clean, and run some boiling water over it. Put the purée into the tray, cool it completely and then freeze. When frozen, you can pop the cubes out if you have a flexible ice cube tray, or pour some boiling water over the back of the tray to loosen them. Put the cubes of purée in a plastic bag, tie it up and label clearly. You can keep these in the freezer for up to two months. To use frozen purée, take one or two cubes out of the freezer and put in a plastic bowl or pot to defrost. Warm purées up to give to your baby, either with warm breast milk or formula or in the microwave. Make sure you stir it through to check there are no hot spots. If you are expressing breast milk, you can freeze this in the same way for adding to food.

Using Pre-Prepared Baby Food

Jars of Food

I generally wouldn't recommend feeding your baby solely on pre-prepared jars of baby food, as they can have a tendency to be bland. Once you are ready to give your baby a mashed version of what you're eating yourself, he may not like it as it will have a lot more flavour. Jars of food can be quite uneconomical, particularly when your baby is just beginning on solids, as there is often a lot left over and they have to be used within twenty-four hours.

However, jars of food can be useful if you don't have time to make something at home or if you're out for the day. If you want to give your baby a quick dessert, jars of fruit purée or chocolate pudding are good. Some very good organic brands of baby food are available.

Packet Baby Food

Packets of dried sweet and savoury baby foods are very good in general, and I would particularly recommend breakfast cereals. Packet foods keep well, and you only need to use a small amount each time, so they tend to be quite economical. They can be made up with warmed breast milk, formula or boiled water. It's a good idea to have some packet food on standby for times when your baby is really hungry, as it can be made up very quickly.

Adding Texture and Variety

From six months of age, you can start to add more texture and different foods to your baby's diet. She will be able to have more or less what the adults and older children are eating, mashed up well. Make sure that it is not very highly seasoned, and if possible take her portion out before you add any extra salt. If you have leftovers from a roast dinner, for example, you can mash them up and freeze them in individual pots ready for your baby.

A good way to start introducing some more texture is to give a mushy cereal such as Weetabix for breakfast. I usually give half a Weetabix to start with, mixed with some breast milk or formula so that the consistency is not too solid. My own children always had a sprinkling of brown sugar on this, but this is entirely up to you.

For lunchtime or evening meals, you can begin to add some meat to your baby's diet. Good first meats to try are cooked chicken, turkey, liver (calves' or chicken) and mince. You will need to mix the meat with some vegetables or baby pasta, and a gravy or sauce to make a soft consistency. Initially you will need to cut the meat up small and mash it with a fork, and as your baby gets bigger he will manage larger pieces. Increasing the lumpiness of his food helps him to practice chewing, and develops the jaw and tongue muscles in preparation for speech.

Your baby can have fish from six months of age, *but not shellfish*. When cooking meals with fish for your baby, make sure you buy filleted fish and *check it carefully for bones after cooking*. You can give your baby fish with a white sauce and mashed potato, or pasta.

Some ideal first meals are shepherd's pie, fish pie, chicken or liver casserole and baby pasta with cheese sauce. Don't be afraid to flavour your baby's food with herbs and spices; for example, some babies love garlic (as long as it's well cooked). Eating foods with plenty of different flavours and textures will be very enjoyable for your baby, and can also help her to get used to having the same kind of food as the rest of the family.

Once your baby is six months old, you can use cow's milk in cooking for him. He can have yoghurts and mild cheese, and well-cooked eggs at this stage too. Scrambled egg is a good meal for suppertime. It's important that your baby has full-fat dairy products at this age, as he needs the fat-soluble vitamins and calories. Don't worry about your baby putting on weight at this stage, as once he starts moving around he will be using up plenty of calories.

Moving on to Finger Food (Six to Twelve Months)

As your baby begins to take an interest in food, she will want to hold food and put her fingers in whatever you're offering her. Don't worry too much about mess at this stage, as it's an important part of development. She needs to explore the feeling of food, but I would stress that you don't have to let food become a plaything. By all means let her try feeding herself with a spoon, but don't let her carry on tipping a bowl of food all over herself or throwing food. When your baby is beginning to feed herself, I find it's a good idea if you have a spoon as well. This enables you to give her plenty of food, and encourage her to have a go as well. Her hands and face will get quite messy during meals, but try not to keep cleaning her up unless she's uncomfortable. Give her a good wash at the end of her meal.

When your baby is ready to start picking up food by himself, rusks and rice cakes are good first finger foods. He will also enjoy bread or toast with butter, jam or Marmite, which you will need to cut up into small pieces. At this stage, it's important that his food is cut up into manageable pieces, and that you sit with him to ensure that he doesn't choke.

Your baby can have soft fruit such as banana, strawberries and grapes, cut up into small pieces, and as she gets more teeth she can have slices of raw vegetables and harder fruit. She will enjoy little pieces of mild cheese, quiche, cold sausages and sliced cold meat. Whenever your child has any finger food, don't leave her unattended.

When your baby is in his highchair, I'd advise that you don't overwhelm him by filling his tray with lots of different pieces of food. To help him get into the routine of family meals, start with a few pieces of savoury food and when he's finished these let him have some sweet things for dessert, such as fruit or cake. Try not to rush your baby's mealtimes, and allow him plenty of time to enjoy his food.

Foods to Avoid

Some foods are unsuitable for younger babies because their digestive system has not developed enough to cope with them. Other foods are not recommended for babies because they could cause an allergic reaction. If you have food allergies or other allergies such as hay fever, asthma or eczema in your family, it is worth being a little more cautious about introducing these foods.

Foods to Avoid under Six Months

For babies under six months old, the following foods should be avoided:

- *wheat products*
- *eggs*
- *cow's milk*
- *meat*
- *fish*
- *citrus fruit or juice.*

Foods to Avoid under Twelve Months

The following should be avoided by babies less than twelve months old:

- *added salt*
- *honey (it can contain a toxin causing botulism)*
- *peanut butter*
- *whole nuts (they should not be given under the age of five)*
- *cow's milk as a drink*
- *shellfish*
- *coffee and tea*
- *alcohol (this should never be given to a child).*

Drinks

Your baby can have cooled boiled water to drink at any age. From about four weeks of age, she can have diluted baby juice in between milk feeds. Once your baby is established in solid feeding, you may find she is more thirsty, and you will need to offer her drinks more often. From twelve months of age, your baby can have full-fat cow's milk, and will also probably need drinks of juice or water during the day.

When to Start Using a Cup

From about three to four months of age, your baby can use a training cup to have drinks. There are many different types of cups and beakers available, with different spouts and lids to prevent spills. Whatever type of beaker or cup you decide to use, your baby will need you to help him drink from it. If you are giving juice or milk in a beaker, try not to let him drink from it throughout the day, as it can fill him up and a constant flow of sugar from milk or juice can damage his teeth.

When to Stop Giving Breast Milk or Formula

When you first introduce solid foods, your baby should continue to have all her normal milk feeds. By the age of six months, she will be having a normal milk feed at about 7.00 a.m. and then solid food plus milk at breakfast, lunch and the evening meal. After the age of six months, you may well find that at lunchtime she is not interested in having any milk after her food. This is perfectly all right, and you can give her a drink of water or baby juice instead. By the time your baby is about nine months old, you can stop giving her milk at 7.00 a.m. and give her a cup of milk with her cereal at breakfast. She can still have a breast or formula feed with her evening meal.

By the time your baby is around twelve months, the aim is for him to be having three meals a day without any breast or formula feeds. From twelve months he can have cow's milk to drink at breakfast and with his evening meal, and juice or water at lunchtime. If your baby has been bottle fed, try to wean him at about twelve months, as it can be difficult to break the habit of drinking from a bottle after this time. It's not a good idea for a toddler to carry a drink around in a bottle or have a bottle in his cot at night, as constant sucking is bad for his teeth.

For more ideas on what to feed your baby, I highly recommend Annabel Karmel's *New Complete Baby and Toddler Meal Planner*, and the section on feeding babies and small children in Nigella Lawson's *How to Eat* (see Further Resources).

CHAPTER 10

Your Baby's Development

You will be amazed at the skills your baby learns and the way she develops in her first year of life. It's hard to imagine your fragile newborn becoming a robust one-year-old, but you will be surprised how quickly this happens. In this chapter, I hope to give you a guide to your baby's development from newborn to twelve months in three-monthly stages. You will find that your baby is an individual and may not do all the things mentioned in each particular section at exactly that time.

It's very easy to become worried by comparing your baby's development with other babies. Parents can often get hung up on whose baby sleeps through the night, or begins teething, crawling, walking or talking first. It's important to remember that each baby and family is different, and your baby's progress is unique to him. Try not to worry if your baby seems to lag behind, but if you are at all concerned speak to your health visitor or doctor.

Your Newborn Baby

Your Baby's Appearance

Many new parents are quite surprised to find that their newborn baby doesn't look as pretty as they expected her to. If you feel this way, don't worry, as she will gradually 'unfold' and begin to look more like a chubby baby in a magazine.

Some newborn babies have quite a misshapen head. This can be due to a long or difficult delivery, or lying awkwardly in the womb. Your baby will have two 'soft spots' or fontanelles on the top of his head, which have given his skull flexibility during birth. The posterior fontanelle at the back of his head is a small opening that will close up by six to eight weeks of age. The anterior fontanelle is larger, and you can often see it pulsing at the top of his head towards the front. This will close by the time he is two years old. It's important to handle your baby's head gently, as the fontanelles are very delicate.

Your baby's nose may initially look quite squashed, her eyes may be puffy and her ears may look bent. You will be surprised how quickly these will sort themselves out, but if you have any concerns after a few weeks, speak to your health visitor. You may notice small pink marks on your baby's forehead, neck or eyelids; these 'stork marks' will fade in a few weeks. Your baby will probably have her eyes closed a lot of the time during the first couple of weeks of life. Most babies are born with blue-grey eyes; however, if they are going to change colour, they will do so by the time she is six months old.

Your baby may have a greasy film on his skin; this is called vernix and has protected his skin in the womb. Vernix is usually greyish-white in colour and odourless. You will often find it under his arms and in any creases in his skin, but it will come off gradually as you bath him over the next couple of weeks. Your baby's skin may also be hairy, which is quite normal. Any hair will usually rub off over the first few days of life.

You may notice that your baby's genitals are quite red and swollen, and both boy and girl babies may have swollen 'breasts'. This is due to the mother's hormones passing to the baby during birth, and will settle down quickly. Your baby's umbilical cord will be a greyish colour and will have a clip on it. The cord will dry up and shrivel quickly and usually drops off within five to ten days.

Your baby's hands and feet may look quite blue and feel cold in the first week to ten days, but this is nothing to worry about, just her circulation settling down. It is a good idea to put socks or bootees on her feet to keep them warm.

Reflexes

All babies are born with a sucking reflex, and are able to swallow too. Your baby will also have a natural instinct to turn his head to the side when he wants food; this is called the rooting reflex. When your baby is rooting, his head will turn to the side and he will open and close his mouth.

If you put your finger in your baby's hand, she has a grasping reflex that makes her curl her fingers around yours and hold on. If you want to lift her arm up, for example to put her cardigan on, let her grasp your finger and she will lift her arm as you gently pull her hand upwards. Up to the age of six weeks, your baby has a stepping reflex, so that if she is held upright above a firm surface she will make stepping movements with her feet.

If your baby feels unsupported when being held or put down, for example to be changed, he may throw out his arms and legs. This is called the startle or Moro reflex. If this happens, make sure to hold your baby securely and put him down gently.

Newborn Checks

Shortly after your baby is born, the doctor or midwife will weigh her and measure her head circumference, and maybe her length. The doctor or midwife will thoroughly examine her, listening to her chest, checking her joints, organs and genitals and making sure she has all the newborn reflexes.

When your baby is about six days old, your health visitor or midwife will take a few drops of blood from his heel for the Guthrie test. This tests for thyroid deficiency and phenylketonuria, which is a rare deficiency in body chemistry. The test is done as a normal procedure, and although your baby won't like it much, he will soon forget if you cuddle and comfort him after the heel prick. If you are breastfeeding, let him feed from you while the midwife takes the sample.

Your Baby at Nought to Three Months

Size and Weight

The average weight of a newborn baby is about 3.4 kg (7 lb 8 oz). You may find that your baby loses weight in the first few days after birth. Fat is stored under the skin, which she will live off for the first few days before the milk comes in. She will normally regain her birth weight by the time she is ten to fourteen days old. After this, your baby will probably gain around 175–225 g (6–8 oz) per week for the first three months of life. If you have any concerns about your baby's weight gain, talk to your health visitor.

Your baby's head circumference will be around 33–39 cm (13–15 inches) at birth, and his head will grow by about 1 cm (0.5 inches) per month for the first five months of life. Your baby's head may look large in comparison with his body, but this is perfectly normal. The average length of a newborn baby is 45–56 cm (17–22 inches), and the first year of life will be his most rapid period of growth.

Routine Check at Six to Eight Weeks

In some areas of the country, when your baby is about six to eight weeks old she will have a full check-up with your health visitor. This is usually done at your local clinic or GP's surgery. The health visitor will check your baby's weight, height and head circumference. She will also look in her mouth and check that her hips are developing well. In some regions, you will also have your postnatal check-up and your baby will have her first set of immunizations at this visit.

Your Baby's Appearance

Nearly all babies develop little white spots on their face and neck in the first few weeks of life. These spots are called milia or milk spots, and are nothing to worry about. Spots are usually caused by the baby's hormones settling down, and the most important thing is not to squeeze them. You may find that they come and go for a while, and will usually disappear after about six weeks. As your baby's body temperature regulates itself, you may find that he gets red, raised heat spots on his face, neck and body. These are temporary and quite normal in the first few weeks of life.

Handle your baby's head gently when washing her hair, as the fontanelle is still quite delicate. Older siblings may be tempted to poke the 'soft spot', so encourage them to be very gentle. If you notice that your baby's anterior fontanelle is sunken, this could well be due to lack of fluids. A bulging fontanelle can be a sign of illness, so if you notice anything unusual, speak to your health visitor or doctor.

Some babies are bald and have no hair until around a year old, whereas others are born with a real thatch. If your baby is born with a lot of hair you will probably find that most of it rubs off in the cot, but don't worry about this, as he will soon grow some more. Your baby's second growth of hair may look quite different from the hair he was born with.

Your baby's arms and legs may look quite skinny for the first few weeks of life, and her feet may turn inwards. Her limbs will gradually fill out as she gains weight, and her legs will straighten over about six weeks. Her fingernails and toenails may be quite long, and you may need to cut her fingernails to prevent her scratching her face.

Physical Development

Your Baby's Senses
When your baby is first born, his eyes can focus best at a distance of about 20–25 cm (8–10 inches). This is designed perfectly so that he can see your face clearly when you are feeding him. You will probably find that your baby is most interested in faces and black and white objects initially, as he can see strong contrasts. In the first few weeks you will notice that he turns his head toward the light.

You may worry that your baby seems to be squinting, or her eyes move in different directions. This is very common as she begins to learn to focus, because her eye muscles are strengthening and becoming co-ordinated. Usually this rights itself by the time your baby is around two months old; however, if you have any concerns talk to your health visitor or doctor. By about three months, your baby will be able to follow your movements around the room with her eyes.

Newborns are very sensitive to sound, and may look startled at loud noises. Your baby will recognize your voice very early on in life, and will respond to you as you talk to him. He will love it when you sing to him, make baby noises and coo. By talking to him, you will find you encourage him to make sounds back to you in baby language. By about two months he will enjoy music, especially musical toys.

Your baby will be born with a sense of taste, and may distinguish different flavours in your milk if you are breastfeeding. Strong flavours may alter the taste of your breast milk, but don't let this worry you unless your baby refuses to feed after you have eaten a particular food. Your baby also has a good sense of smell, and will recognize your smell early on in life. She can smell your milk and will root, turning her head towards your breast. Babies usually have this rooting reflex for the first three to four months of life.

143

Your baby will love to be touched and held close and will enjoy skin-to-skin contact, lying with his tummy on your stomach or chest. You will probably find that your baby is very content when he is held gently but securely in your arms. Being clothed in warm, comfortable clothes will also make him happy, and he may cry in the early days when he is undressed. Newborn babies often don't like being in water, and will have a good shout when bathed. By the time your baby is about two weeks old, you will probably find he is beginning to enjoy the feeling of water on his skin and loves this special time with you.

Breathing

You will notice that your newborn baby breathes very quickly when she's awake, but as she gets older, her breathing will become slower. You may find that your baby sneezes a lot in the early days, but this is quite normal and usually doesn't mean she has a cold or hay fever. Sneezing helps her to clear her nose and air passages as she gets used to life outside the womb.

When your baby is asleep his breathing will be slower, and if he's in a very deep sleep it can be difficult to see him breathing at all. Some babies make very little noise when they sleep, whereas others are quite snuffly, and may sound like little pigs! If your baby is a noisy sleeper, this will improve over the early months.

Digestion

You will probably notice that your baby hiccups a lot, either during feeding or between feeds. Don't be alarmed by hiccups, as they are quite normal and don't hurt her at all; in fact, she probably hiccupped in your womb before birth. After feeding, your baby will usually have wind, and may bring up a little bit of her feed (posseting). Again, this is perfectly normal, and some babies bring up more milk than others.

Your baby will usually urinate in the first few hours after birth. Once he is feeding well, you will find he produces lots of wet nappies, which shows his kidneys are working. If you're not sure whether he is weeing, take his nappy off and you will often find that the change in temperature makes him wee. If your baby is not producing wet nappies, this may be due to a lack of fluids. If the urine has a strong smell, or if there is blood in it, you need to contact your health visitor.

Your baby's first bowel movements will be meconium, which is dark green and sticky. This will appear for about two or three days, until her bowels have cleared. In a breastfed baby, normal stools will be frothy, quite runny and yellowish in colour. Bottle-fed babies' stools will be firmer and yellow. Some babies poo at every feed, and the poo can be quite runny and may squirt out of the nappy – so be prepared! Other babies only poo twice a day, and this is normal too. At about two months of age you may find that your baby suddenly goes for a couple of days without a dirty nappy. This is quite normal, and does not mean she is constipated. I have found that babies who start having formula at around two months of age may go for several days without a dirty nappy. If your baby is straining to pass a motion and her stools are hard like rabbit droppings, then she is probably constipated. Your baby's poo will become more solid as she gets older, usually when she starts having some solid food.

Physical Skills

At birth, your baby can turn his head from side to side but he cannot yet lift his head or support its weight. When picking him up and carrying him, make sure that you support his head and neck with your hand or arm. His muscle tone and co-ordination are not yet fully developed, and you will find that he moves his arms and legs quite jerkily in the early weeks.

By the time your baby is around two months old, she will be holding her head up more on her own, and will feel much firmer and stronger when you pick her up. She will have lost her newborn look and jerkiness. You will probably find that she loves having her nappy off and having a good kick. From about six to eight weeks she will enjoy kicking and stretching under a baby gym. By three months, she may be beginning to reach out to touch hanging toys, and clasping things with her hands.

Social Development

You and your baby will spend lots of time getting to know each other in the early weeks of life. He soon recognizes your voice and smell, and the way you hold and handle him. Feeding is a very important part of his day, as he enjoys the close contact and cuddles, and hearing you talk to him. Gradually your baby will start to respond to you by gazing at your face, making faces and smiling from about four weeks onwards. You may find that your baby makes his first smile if you tickle him around his mouth after a feed when he's full and contented.

Once your baby is around two to three months old you will notice a big change in her social skills. She will be much happier to have wakeful times, not just wanting to be fed. She will happily sit in a bouncy chair and watch what you are doing. She will begin to smile and make cooing noises, and by three months she will probably gurgle and blow bubbles. She will be more responsive when you talk to her, and take an interest in other siblings. You will also find that she notices new people, and may become shy or cry when introduced to somebody new.

Your Baby at Three to Six Months

Weight

At around three months, your baby's weight gain will slow down and he will probably gain about 500 g (1 lb) per month until he is a year old. By the time he is six months old, your baby will probably be about double his birth weight. If your baby has not been gaining enough weight, your health visitor will give you support and advice when you take him to the clinic.

Physical Development

Teething

Your baby is born with the foundations of two sets of teeth. The first set or 'milk teeth' are formed early in pregnancy, and the second set, of adult teeth, are formed in the later months. Your baby may start teething as early as three months old, but normally the teeth don't appear until she is at least six months old. The first sign of teething is dribbling, and you may notice that your baby has a red cheek. She may also have loose stools and a sore bottom and you will probably also find that she is more fractious than usual. Teething pain can go on for some weeks before the first tooth actually appears. The first teeth to cut are the front incisors, both top and bottom, and once these have appeared she will have four teeth in the front.

When your baby is teething, you can use teething granules, gel or teething rings to soothe the pain. He can also have infant paracetamol, which will help him to sleep, particularly if teething pain is waking him at night. You will probably find that your baby has good and bad days when he's teething, and once the tooth comes through he will settle down again.

Physical Skills
Between three and six months, you will notice a marked change in your baby's development as she becomes stronger and more mobile. When put on her tummy she will be able to hold her head up well. You will find that you don't need to support her head so much when you carry her, but make sure you still hold her securely, as she can throw herself back quite strongly.

By four months of age, your baby may be able to roll from his back onto his side, and before long will be rolling right over onto his tummy. He will enjoy nappy-free kick times on his changing mat on the floor. By the time your baby is around six months old, he will be able to sit up for a little while, supported by pillows or cushions. If you stand your baby up, held securely around the waist, he will plant his feet firmly on your lap or the floor but his body will still be quite wobbly. He will love to practise this movement, but will need plenty of support from you.

From around four to six months of age your baby will be developing the skills to reach for and grab toys with both hands. When you hand her something to hold she will try very hard to take it from you. This grabbing and holding movement will become easier for her as she learns to become co-ordinated. She will also hold and shake a rattle when given one, and everything will go into her mouth. At this stage you will need to be careful that she doesn't put anything in her mouth that could harm her. During this time she will have found her hands, and will spend long periods holding them in front of her and looking at them intently, as if wondering what they are. When she is lying on her back kicking she will play with her feet too, even trying to put them in her mouth.

During this period, you will probably be starting your baby on solid food. He will have a good appetite and will get very excited when he sees his food or bottle coming. Once he has been having solid food for a little while, he will want to take the spoon when you are feeding him, and will be beginning to show signs of independence. He will also be learning to spit food out, so beware!

Social Development

Your baby will be responding well to singing and talking, and will love you singing songs and nursery rhymes to her. She may start imitating you, which can be very funny. She will love games with rhythm, like 'This little piggy went to market' and 'Round and round the garden'. You will generally find that she is happy and contented, gurgling and giggling and learning to make all sorts of noises. She will also begin to take an interest in books; if you buy board books, she can't tear them up or chew them to pieces easily. She will be taking more notice of her surroundings and will love having her toys around her. Try not to overwhelm her with too many toys, as she will be quite content with just a few at this age.

From around three months your baby will be noticing new faces well, and you may find that he is quite shy with new people. He will respond quickly to loud noises, and will sometimes cry if frightened. He may also cry when you walk out of the room, as he is becoming much more aware of your movements and his need for company. You will begin to notice that, when your baby is sleepy, he will rub his eyes, yawn and turn his head away. If he sucks his thumb, he will put it in his mouth as soon as he is tired. If he has a cuddly blanket he will be very attached to it by now.

Your Baby at Six to Nine Months

Routine Tests

When your baby is about eight months old she will have a medical check-up, which will be done at your local clinic by your health visitor. She will check your baby's weight, height and head circumference. She will also look at her hips, check for a squint and check her mobility. If there are any problems she will refer you to your doctor. At around nine months your baby will also have her first routine hearing test.

Physical Development

By the time your baby is six months old his eyes will be able to focus well, and if they are going to change colour they will have done so by now. You will notice that he will move himself round so that he can see things, and he will watch you coming in and out of the room. From around six months your baby will be able to sit up with the help of cushions. Without cushions he will fall backwards or forwards, as his back is still not strong enough to support him. From around seven to nine months, he will gradually be able to sit up with less support.

Some babies start crawling during this time, either on their tummies or shuffling along on their bottoms. If you lie on the floor with your baby, you can encourage her to crawl towards you, offering her a toy as she gets close to you. She will now be able to hold things in her fingers, and co-ordination of both hands will be better. She will be able to clap her hands too, and may pass objects from one hand to the other.

Your baby will have much more variety in his diet by the time he is nine months old. He will enjoy feeding himself with small pieces of finger food and will want to feed himself with a spoon, although he will still need quite a lot of help. During this period, he will be able to drink from a cup, and will probably want to hold it himself.

Social Development

By the time your baby is six to nine months old, you will notice that she is becoming much more vocal. She will be repeating sounds such as 'ma-ma' and 'da-da', but won't understand their meaning yet. She will still enjoy rhyming games such as 'pat-a-cake' and 'peepo', and will respond to you with giggles. She will also be learning to communicate with you physically, for example by lifting her arms up to be picked up or held, and pointing to things.

At this age, your baby will be fascinated by almost everything that you do. He will often be quite happy to sit in his highchair or pushchair and watch you as you prepare meals or do the ironing or gardening. Unless your baby is having an off day with teething, you will find that he is happy and contented for longer periods, amusing himself with his toys or just watching family life. Outside the family, you may find that he is more clingy and shy, and wants to be held and picked up more for comfort, particularly if he is tired.

Your Baby at Nine to Twelve Months

Weight

By the time your baby is a year old, she will probably be about three times her birth weight. The average height for a one-year-old is around 72 cm (28 inches); however, babies vary enormously in their growth rate and height, so don't worry if your baby seems much taller or shorter than her friends.

Physical Development

By the time your baby is twelve months old he will probably have eight teeth, and by two years he will have his full set of twenty teeth. It's a good idea for him to have his own toothbrush and toothpaste, although he will still need help with cleaning his teeth. His muscles will be stronger and much more controlled, and he will be able to lift his head up when you lay him down. He will be able to see at greater distances, and will follow objects easily with his eyes.

By nine months of age your baby should be sitting up well without support. She will probably now be crawling around well, and you will need to keep a constant eye on her for her safety. If you are using a playpen, it will become invaluable at this stage. Your baby may begin to pull herself up by holding onto the furniture and will be able to stand for a short time. By the time she is a year old, she may shuffle sideways supporting herself on the furniture, and will enjoy walking towards you as you hold her hands. Your baby's first step is very exciting, and babies differ in the age at which they start to walk. You don't need to worry if your baby is not walking by a year old, as some babies do not walk until around twenty-one months.

Your baby will have good control over his hands and fingers, and by the time he is a year old he may be able to hold a pencil or crayon, and throw a ball. He will enjoy stacking blocks and playing with bricks, and will have favourite toys at this stage. He will also love listening to music, and will often 'dance' along to familiar songs.

Playtime will be a big part of his life, and he will enjoy copying grown-up activities such as using a toy dustpan and brush.

Your baby should be eating and sleeping well by the time she is a year old. It's a good idea to wean her off the breast or bottle at around twelve months, as it can become more difficult as she gets older. She will often show excitement at mealtimes, but may well shut her eyes and shake her head at you if she doesn't want her food. When she is in her highchair make sure she is strapped in, as at this stage she is very mobile and can topple out easily. You will probably find that socializing with your baby becomes much easier, as when you go out she can have what you are having to eat.

Social Development

By the time your baby is around a year old, he will have become a very social little person. His world will have expanded beyond the immediate family, particularly if he is going to playgroup or a day nursery. He will recognize people he sees often, and may wave hello and goodbye. He will understand a lot of what you are saying, and will respond to some of your requests. Chatting to him about what you are doing each day will help his speech develop. His speech will probably be increasing rapidly, and he will begin to repeat easy words. You will often find that 'No' is one of the first words he says, closely followed by 'Mummy' and 'Daddy'. Again, don't worry if your baby is not talking much at twelve months, as some babies start much later than others.

Playing and interacting with adults is very important for your baby at this stage in her development. Older siblings will also provide lots of entertainment and fun for your baby, and it's lovely to see them giggling and playing together. By about twelve months your baby will love to get involved in household jobs, for example using her own duster or helping you to unpack the shopping. She will learn a huge amount from watching and copying you in everyday life. She will want to have kitchen utensils to play with, such as plastic boxes and wooden spoons, but make sure that anything you give her to play with is safe.

You may well find that by the time your baby is a year old, he is quite strong-willed and has occasional tantrums; this is perfectly normal. You may feel that you spend most of your days saying 'No!' to your baby, but setting boundaries is an important part of growing up. Many parents find it's easier to remove anything that they don't want their baby to touch, but this only provides a temporary solution. In my experience, helping your baby to know what he should and shouldn't do at home will enable him to mix with other children and adults much more easily. The most important thing is to say 'Yes' and encourage your baby as much as possible, so that he learns that your attention is focused on his successes and good behaviour.

As you look back over the first year of life, you will be amazed at the changes that have happened to your baby. The first year is a time to be treasured, and it will go by very quickly. In writing this book, it's been very enjoyable to read the diaries I kept about our children, and to remember the fun we all had at different stages. You could keep a scrapbook or diary of your baby's first year, and of course plenty of photos, which will be a delight for your family to look back on over the years.

CHAPTER 11

Common Illnesses

The vast majority of babies will have a mild infection or illness at some stage during their first year of life. As parents, our natural instinct is to want to protect our baby from any illnesses, and it can be very distressing when a baby is ill. It is very natural to feel anxious about illness in your baby, and many parents feel unsure about when they should contact the doctor. This chapter aims to help you to recognize the symptoms of common illnesses, and to advise you about the treatment you can give at home and when you should contact a health professional. It is very important to stress that this is not intended to replace medical advice, and if you have any concerns about your baby's health do not hesitate to contact your doctor or health visitor straight away.

Your baby will be offered a number of immunizations (vaccinations) from the age of eight weeks to give her immunity against serious childhood illnesses. I always advise parents to go ahead with all vaccinations offered, as the long-term consequences of illnesses such as measles, mumps and rubella can be extremely serious, whereas the immunizations are extremely safe. Talk to your doctor or health visitor if you have any worries.

Jaundice

Many babies have some jaundice in the early days of life, which is caused by immature functioning of the liver and is not normally a serious condition. Your baby's skin and the whites of his eyes will have a yellowish tinge if he has jaundice. This colour will come and go, some days being more pronounced than others. Jaundiced babies will normally be very sleepy, and you will usually have to wake them up to feed. Jaundice can last for up to two to three weeks and resolves itself as your baby's liver develops.

You can treat jaundice yourself by making sure that your baby sleeps in normal sunlight as much as possible, ensuring that she doesn't overheat. Your health visitor will keep an eye on your baby's jaundice in the early weeks, and in rare cases your baby may need to be re-admitted to hospital for treatment. Hospital treatment usually involves putting your baby under a bright ultra-violet light. In very rare cases a baby with severe jaundice might need medical intervention, and this is especially true if her urine is unusually yellow and/or her stools always pale or white.

Gastro-reflux

Gastro-reflux is caused by a weaker than usual sphincter muscle between the stomach and oesophagus (gullet). This means that the stomach is less able to hold milk, causing vomiting, which then irritates the oesophagus and throat. Gastro-reflux is more common in boys than girls, and seems to happen more often in large, hungry babies.

Babies will not normally show symptoms of gastro-reflux until around four weeks of age. The main symptom is vomiting; this will not necessarily happen at every feed, but may happen more than once between feeds. You may also find that your baby brings up vomit in his cot after a feed. Vomiting will usually happen whether he has had a large or small feed. Projectile vomiting is much more powerful than the normal possetting of small amounts of milk during or after a feed, and can be caused by feeding on top of wind. However, sustained projectile vomiting soon after feeds may be a sign of a different problem.

A baby with gastro-reflux may show signs of discomfort during feeding, and may pull away from the breast or bottle after her initial hunger is satisfied. Her throat and oesophagus may be sore, and she may pull up her legs after a feed, due to pain in her stomach. After a feed, you may hear her stomach gurgling, and hear a gulping noise in her throat before she vomits. She can also sound quite chesty, as if she has catarrh when she is sleeping. If your baby does have severe gastro-reflux, she will often begin to lose weight and will be hungry and unsettled between feeds.

Get in touch with your health visitor or GP if your baby is vomiting a lot and you think he may have gastro-reflux. If your baby is bottle fed your GP will usually recommend a thicker, more solid formula feed. He may also prescribe an antacid for breast and bottle-fed babies. This treatment will usually resolve mild gastro-reflux, but if your baby continues to vomit or lose weight you may need to see your doctor again.

If your baby has gastro-reflux, try not to move her around a lot during and after a feed. When you wind her, sit her up carefully and don't jiggle her too much. If she is vomiting regularly, you will find you need to change her clothes and wash her more often. It can be disheartening if your baby has reflux, as feed times can be quite stressful. However, don't despair, as you will often find that starting solids helps, and by the time she is a year old her symptoms will have disappeared.

Colic or Wind

Many parents are afraid that their baby will have colic. The word 'colic' is very emotive, and is often used to describe a crying, unsettled baby who can't be comforted. If your baby is well fed at regular three- to four-hour intervals and is winded well, his crying is unlikely to be due to colic.

If your baby cries, screams and draws up her knees during or after a feed, she might have stomach pain due to trapped wind. Babies' intestines are small and still developing, so air swallowed during feeding can cause discomfort as it goes down. If your baby screams and seems in great pain during a feed, keep as calm as you can. Take your baby off the breast or bottle, put her on your shoulder and spend a little time rubbing her back to try to get all her wind up. If you are bottle feeding your baby, make sure that you are holding the bottle so that the teat is always filled with milk. This will help to prevent your baby swallowing any air. You may also find it helps to try anti-colic teats and bottles. Some parents find it helpful to try Infacol drops or gripe water; however, I advise that feeding at regular intervals and winding properly helps best.

If your baby seems to be in a lot of pain at every feed, you should take him to see the doctor and talk about your concerns. If you are bottle feeding, your doctor may advise that you change to a dairy-free formula. Your doctor may also prescribe medication to ease the discomfort of trapped wind.

Recent studies have shown that much crying after feeds is actually habit and that if it results in lots of holding and cuddling it is likely to continue for much longer. Doctors now suggest picking babies up only very briefly when they are crying, and once you have made reassuring murmurings and given them a short cuddle you should put them back down even if they are still crying (see Chapter 7). It has been shown that this results in a quicker recovery from 'colic' than anything else.

Eye Infections

Runny Eyes or Conjunctivitis

Babies' normal eye secretions are initially yellow after birth and then become clear like tears. However, some babies get eye infections in the early days after birth, due to bacteria picked up from the birth canal. To treat runny eyes, ensure that you clean your baby's eyes with cooled boiled water, using a separate cotton ball for each eye. When cleaning your baby's eyes, wipe from the inside corner by the nose towards the outer corner. If your baby's eyes are stuck together with a thick green mucus or are clearly red and inflamed, it is likely to be an infection. In the case of an eye infection, contact your GP, who can prescribe eye drops to treat it.

Blocked Tear Ducts

If your baby's eyes look more watery than usual, she may have a blocked tear duct. These usually clear up by themselves, so make sure that you clean her eyes with cooled boiled water as above.

Coughs, Colds and Chest Infections

If your baby has a cold, he will often sneeze for a few days, and then have a runny nose. He may be quite miserable, and may cough and have some difficulty breathing and feeding. If he has a chest infection, his temperature will also be slightly raised. Your baby's temperature should normally be between 36 and 37 °C (96.8 and 98.6 °F).

You can treat coughs and colds at home with a decongestant rub, capsules or linctus suitable for babies. You can also give Calpol or a similar paracetamol-based infant medicine to bring down your baby's temperature. Make sure when giving any medicine to young babies that you have checked the label to find out what age it can be given from. Give your baby plenty of cooled boiled water if she is under two months, or baby juice if she is older, particularly if she is having difficulty feeding. If your baby is distressed and not feeding, or if her temperature remains high, contact your doctor.

Croup

Croup is a harsh, rasping, wheezy cough caused by an infection of the chest or, less commonly, the epiglottis (the valve in the throat shutting off the windpipe). If your baby has croup he may sound hoarse, and his throat will sound quite tight. You can treat croup yourself by sitting your baby in a steamy room and giving him plenty to drink. If your baby has a fever or changes colour, contact your GP as soon as possible for advice.

Ear Infections

If your baby has an ear infection she will often have a hot, red ear, and older babies may pull or rub their ear. She will be quite fretful and will probably have a raised temperature. It is important to contact your doctor as soon as possible if your baby has an ear infection, and you may be prescribed antibiotics in liquid form. Untreated middle ear infections can cause severe pain and burst eardrums in babies. When you take your baby swimming she may get an infection of the outer ear canal, which can be even more painful, but is usually treated with eardrops rather than oral antibiotics.

Raised Temperature

If your baby has a temperature he will be hot, flushed and sweaty. He may also be quite sleepy or miserable. If you take your baby's temperature using an ear or forehead thermometer and it is above 38 °C (100.4 °F), he has a fever. You can normally reduce a fever by giving a paracetamol suspension such as Calpol from one month old, or an ibuprofen-based medicine if he is over six months old.

Give plenty of fluids, and don't worry if he goes off his food. You can also cool him down by making sure he doesn't have too many clothes on, and sponging his head or body with tepid water and allowing it to evaporate. Don't put your baby in a draught, but make sure his room is not too hot. If you check your baby's temperature every three to four hours, and it is not coming down after twenty-four hours, contact your doctor. If your baby is clearly unwell, with a temperature but cold hands and feet or a bluish tinge, call your doctor immediately as this may suggest a serious infection.

In rare cases, if your baby's temperature increases suddenly she can have febrile convulsions, in which her arms and legs jerk and she may possibly lose consciousness. If you see signs of a febrile convulsion, lay your baby in a safe place propped up in the first-aid recovery position, and call your doctor or an ambulance.

Cradle Cap

Cradle cap is scaly, yellowish patches on your baby's scalp or forehead, which can develop at any time during the first few months of life. It is caused by a build-up of dead skin and is nothing to worry about, as it is easy to treat at home. Put some baby oil or olive oil on cotton wool, and rub it gently in circular movements onto the patches of cradle cap. You can leave the oil on overnight, and wash off gently with baby shampoo the next day. Repeat this process until the cradle cap softens and disappears, but don't pick at it as this can cause irritation and infection.

Eczema

If your baby has the common, atopic form of eczema, you may initially notice patches of dry skin in the folds of his arms, knees, hands and wrists. This usually develops into an itchy, reddish rash, which can come and go in mild cases. Eczema can occur from around the age of two to three months, often when babies are teething. Eczema is often partly hereditary, so if other members of your family have suffered from eczema, look out for early signs in your baby.

If you suspect your baby has eczema, take her to the doctor to confirm this. Your doctor may prescribe an emollient such as aqueous cream, and Oilatum liquid for the bath. If your baby has eczema, it is important not to use ordinary soap or baby wash on her skin. If the initial treatment does not work, your doctor will probably prescribe a steroid cream to use on sore patches. These creams are quite safe if used according to medical advice, but if you want to use them less you need to concentrate on the emollient creams.

You may find that pet hair and dust can exacerbate eczema, so you may need to vacuum more often and keep pets away from your baby's room. Make sure that you use a non-biological washing powder and avoid woollen clothing to prevent further irritation to your baby's skin. Cotton clothing is usually the best, and avoiding overheating can help to reduce itchiness from eczema. If your baby has very bad eczema, you can buy a cotton all-in-one night suit with mittens attached, which will help to prevent him scratching his skin. Avoiding all dairy products in your baby's diet may also help to alleviate eczema. In my experience, many children grow out of infantile eczema.

Rashes

Heat rashes are the most common skin rashes in young babies. If your baby has a heat rash, she will have little raised spots around the back of her neck or shoulders. Her skin will feel hot and look quite pink, and she may be uncomfortable. To treat heat rash, remove some of her covers or clothes to cool her down slowly.

When your baby starts teething and is dribbling more than usual, you may find that the skin around his mouth and neck becomes red and sore. This happens because his skin is frequently wet with saliva, which can cause irritation. To help soothe and heal this, use a gentle baby moisturising cream or E45 cream.

Nappy Rash

Prevention is better than cure with nappy rash, so make sure that you change your baby's nappy frequently, and keep her bottom clean and dry. However, the vast majority of babies will get nappy rash at some stage. If your baby has mild nappy rash, her bottom will look a little red. More severe nappy rash will be very sore, and her bottom will have broken skin and look a very angry red colour.

Mild nappy rash will clear up quickly if you use a good medicated barrier cream such as Sudacrem, and leave your baby's nappy off with his bottom exposed to the air to dry it after changing. With more severe nappy rash, you may need to contact your doctor and get a stronger cream such as Metanium.

Thrush

Thrush is an infection caused by a yeast called *Candida albicans*. Normally, thrush occurs in the mouth in young babies. If you notice small white spots in your baby's mouth and her tongue looks red and sore, she may well have thrush. Thrush makes feeding painful and difficult for babies, and you will probably find that she pulls away from the breast or bottle even when she is hungry. You may find that your baby is more susceptible to thrush if you are breastfeeding and have had a course of antibiotics after the birth. This is because antibiotics can kill the bacteria that naturally suppress *Candida* in the body. Thrush on your nipples can also be passed on to your baby. Your baby can also get thrush on her bottom; if so, her bottom will look red with small white spots. This will not clear up by simply airing her bottom and using Sudacrem, and you will need to see your doctor.

If you or your baby have thrush anywhere, it's important to make sure that you wash your hands before and after contact with your baby. You will need to contact your doctor, who will give you a course of treatment; this usually clears up the infection within a few days.

Constipation

If your baby is constipated his poo will look hard and solid like rabbit droppings, and he will strain hard when dirtying his nappy. He may also cry when doing a poo, and in severe cases there may be some bleeding if his skin tears around the anus. Don't worry that your baby is constipated if he doesn't poo for a few days and then produces a large dirty nappy that is normal in colour and texture.

The most important thing in treating constipation is to give your baby plenty of cooled boiled water, to which you can add up to a teaspoon of brown sugar per 110 ml (4 fl oz). You can also give her prune juice or fruit juice from four weeks of age, or if she's eating solids, give more fruit and vegetables. If your baby's constipation lasts for more than a few days, or if you are at all concerned, contact your doctor.

Diarrhoea

Diarrhoea is quite different from a normal breastfed baby's poo, which tends to be loose and frothy. If your baby has diarrhoea, his poo will be loose, very watery and a greenish-yellow colour. He will dirty his nappy very frequently, even if it's just a small amount. He will probably be quite fretful and uncomfortable. Sometimes your baby will have vomiting as well as diarrhoea, often due to a stomach infection.

Your baby can dehydrate quickly when she has diarrhoea. If you are breastfeeding, continue to feed and give her extra drinks of cooled boiled water, and if you are bottle feeding you can dilute the formula more than usual. If diarrhoea persists, consult your doctor.

Urinary Infections

Urinary infections are uncommon in babies under one year old; girls are more susceptible than boys, due to bacteria travelling up the urethra into the bladder. If your baby's urine smells very strong, and she appears to be in discomfort when weeing or has an unexplained fever, she may have a urinary infection. Give plenty of fluids and see your doctor, who will do a urine test and may prescribe antibiotics.

Bites and Stings

Stings from insects such as bees, wasps and mosquitoes can cause a lot of discomfort to your baby. If your baby has been stung or bitten, he will have a red mark and an itchy raised swelling on his skin. If a bee has stung your baby, you may see the sting still in his skin; you can carefully remove this with tweezers. Soothe his skin with anti-sting cream or give him an anti-histamine medicine suitable for babies. If your baby is stung in his mouth or throat and it is beginning to swell, take him straight to a hospital, because once the area swells up it will affect his breathing very quickly.

Burns and Scalds

If your baby's skin is scalded with hot liquid or burned on a hot surface, cool the area immediately with plenty of cold running water. If possible, keep the area under running water for fifteen to twenty minutes. Your baby's skin will look red and may blister. Once it is cool, you can cover the skin with a smooth (non-fluffy) fabric dressing; don't use sticking plaster. If the burn covers more than a few centimetres or if you are at all concerned about it once you have cooled it down, take your baby to the doctor or a hospital.

Cuts and Grazes

Once your baby is learning to walk, she will be likely to get cuts and grazes on her knees and hands when she overbalances. Clean cuts and grazes very gently with water and cotton wool, and put on some antiseptic cream, such as Savlon, to prevent infection and aid healing. It is usually best to leave the area open to the air rather than using a plaster or dressing, unless it is bleeding heavily. Most minor cuts and grazes will heal within a few days.

Bronchiolitis

Upper and lower respiratory infections (affecting the breathing tubes from nose to lungs) are relatively common and are usually mild virus infections. The commonest would be 'wheezy bronchitis'. The most typical causes for noisy breathing are non-infectious. However, breathing problems will result in breathlessness, difficulty in feeding, rapid laboured breathing, and a change of skin colour; this will require medical attention, sometimes urgently. Bronchiolitis often occurs in infancy, usually during the winter months.

CHAPTER 12

Family Life

Family life is the foundation of society everywhere in the world, producing enrichment and stability. It is a privilege as parents to develop and nurture a new generation, and to instil confidence in your child in his worth and value. When you first look at your tiny baby, it's exciting to think that he will have a unique role to play in his own generation as he grows up. The love and care that we can give to our children in family life will enable them to grow into people who know how to care for one another in society. Becoming parents, however, is the biggest challenge that most couples will face, so it is important to give some thought as to how you will meet this challenge, both as parents and as a couple.

When parents separate it often brings pain and heartache, not only to the couple involved but to the children too. This can be felt in the lives of those it has touched, sometimes for years, and often the pain never goes away. On the other hand, it is important to recognize that in situations of extreme conflict, especially involving violence, separating can be beneficial for both children and parents. However, parenting is much harder for a single parent than for a couple who can work as a team to achieve a good parenting partnership. From my own experience of divorce and remarriage to my original husband, I feel passionate about the importance of a stable family environment, and know that children really do thrive in it.

In this chapter, I hope to suggest some practical ideas to help integrate your baby into family life. We also look at some of the joys and challenges of becoming parents, including the new relationship with your own parents and in-laws. Finally, we look at how to help your children have good relationships with their siblings and grandparents.

Integrating Your Baby into Family Life

Having a baby will inevitably bring changes to your life as a couple and your wider family life. When you have a baby, there are often things you will have to give up or change for a while. However, it's important to strike a balance so that the whole family don't feel they have to drop everything to accommodate the new addition.

Many new parents find that they run their lives around their baby, often because they feel she needs twenty-four-hour attention. In the early days, many parents are unsure what their baby's needs are, and can become pretty frazzled trying to sort out what they should do to make her happy. In my experience, parents who are on the go constantly find that their baby becomes more fractious, they become more tense and family life in general suffers. In contrast, parents who are able to put their baby down in her pram or cot and make some time for themselves often find the demands of a new baby easier to cope with.

Many of the families I've worked with have asked me how to help fit their new baby into family life. Having a flexible routine enables you to plan when your baby will sleep and feed, and gives you the freedom to fit time for yourself and the family into the day. Leaving your baby to settle himself rather than picking him up each time he cries will give you much more time and freedom. A routine and structure helps your baby to feel more settled and secure, and he will learn to sleep better if he is given time to settle himself rather than being constantly picked up. As parents, you won't feel that every waking moment is spent attending to your baby, and you'll have time to get on with your domestic routine and other commitments. Your baby has a right to be loved, nurtured and cared for, but not to believe he will always be the centre of the universe.

If you are going to use the flexible routine I describe in Chapter 6, then you will probably have to make some sacrifices. Making sure that your baby has her sleep and feed at the right time will mean that there are times of the day when you cannot just drop everything and go out. I can only assure you that this will pay off in the long run, and you will be very pleased when you have a baby who generally sleeps and feeds when you want her to. Your baby will benefit from this too; it is a joy to see babies thriving and being happy and contented when they are into a good routine.

As your baby settles into family life, you will find that you have more time to give to each other and to your other children. As parents, it's important to spend time together deciding what boundaries you are going to set as your baby gets older, and agreeing on your approach to parenting. Unity between you as parents will enable you to support one another and help your child to grow up feeling secure.

Becoming Parents

Your Relationship with Your Parents and In-laws

When you have a new baby, you share an experience with your own parents and you may find you suddenly understand more about what they did and thought as parents. However, it can be hard to take advice about bringing up your baby from your parents or in-laws. If possible, try to build a healthy balance, where you are willing to learn from their wisdom but are free to make your own choices.

As a woman, the experience of childbirth can bring you closer to your own mother, as you now understand the depth of maternal love much more. Becoming a mother often brings a new bond with your own mother, as you have more to share. Sadly, sometimes having a baby causes tension, particularly if you don't have a good relationship with your own mother.

Your relationship as a couple with your in-laws will probably change after the birth of your baby. If you've not seen much of them before, you may find you're in more regular contact, as often babies bring the wider family together. It's important to communicate with your in-laws and let them know how important they are to you and your baby. Although you may find you want to set boundaries about how often you see one another, it's important that both your parents and in-laws don't feel excluded.

Some new parents struggle with unwanted advice from their own parents or in-laws, particularly in the early days. If you feel your parents or in-laws are interfering, try gently and calmly to tell them that you and your partner would rather do it your own way. It's much better to discuss this sooner rather than later, to avoid tension building up. The most important thing to remember is that you, your partner and baby are a new family unit and you need time to adjust.

The Joys of Being a Dad

I can't emphasize enough how important dads are in a family. Nowadays, fathers are often undervalued and their role can be undermined, in a society which pressurizes mothers to 'be everything'. For me personally, my own father has been a stabilizing influence throughout the whole of my life. Even though a father may find that he doesn't have much of a hands-on role with his baby, particularly in the early weeks of life, he shouldn't underestimate his importance in the family unit. His partner will need him as she adjusts to motherhood, and he can provide vital emotional and practical support for both his partner and child.

For you as a first-time dad, there is a real joy in holding your newborn baby in your arms. You may feel overwhelmed by a huge sense of responsibility, but also excited about the future. You may have longed for this baby, and you will feel very proud if you are told he looks just like you. As a dad, you have an important role to play in protecting your partner and newborn, and you may be surprised how strong these feelings are in the early weeks. Your support and practical help will be invaluable to your partner, and getting involved with bathing, changing and settling your baby will help you to develop a deep bond with him.

As your child grows, you can often help her to take healthy risks in life, whereas mothers can be more protective. For young children, rough-and-tumble play with dad helps develop physical skills and a sense of fun. You can help to boost your child's confidence in her own abilities, such as learning to ride a bike, playing ball games or helping with the gardening. You can also give unconditional love, making your child feel special by praising her for who she is, not what she's done. One friend described to me the way her granddaughter had benefited from her dad's love: 'He wants her to know from the start that there's a man in her life who thinks she's just the bee's knees.'

The Challenges of Being a Dad

In the early days of your baby's life, you may not feel a huge rush of love for him. Don't let this worry you, as many fathers find that their love for their baby grows as he gets older and a bit more interesting.

Many fathers feel quite inadequate in meeting the needs of their newborn and partner, and may feel squeezed out by the intensity of the new relationship between mother and baby. You may find that at times you feel angry, resentful or jealous, particularly if your partner is breastfeeding. It can be hard to adjust to having another person in the house, not just you and your partner any more.

Initially, it can be quite hard to understand that your partner is completely taken up with the new baby, and she may just want to cuddle him and not want you near her. Try to remember that her hormones are all over the place after birth, and that the closeness between you as a couple will return: just give it time. You will both need to adjust to your new roles as parents as well as lovers.

You are going to feel tired after the birth of your baby, as watching your partner go through childbirth can be very emotionally draining. Ongoing broken nights and returning to work can also add to your exhaustion. If you are back at work, don't feel guilty about moving into a spare room so that you can have a full night's sleep; it is important that you are able to cope during the day. Many couples find that they can share the night feeds over the weekend, to give the mother some time to catch up on sleep.

If both you and your partner were working before your baby was born, you may find it very stressful adjusting to being the sole financial provider for a time. You may also find that your employer is not very understanding about the demands of a new baby, and you are still expected to work long hours and maintain your performance at work. Balancing work and home-life demands is very challenging, and many fathers feel they don't see their children for enough time during the day. Days off and holidays together as a family are very important, giving you more quality time to spend with your partner and children.

The Joys of Being a Mum

Just before I wrote this chapter, my own mother died very suddenly. The impact on me has been very emotional, and it has caused me once again to look at the importance of families, and the effect our mothers have on us. In my case, my mother left a legacy to us as a family of how important we all are to each other.

Often a new mother will experience a sense of deep fulfilment as a woman in having a baby. During pregnancy you become more conscious of the instinct to protect and nurture the baby growing within you, and you may be overwhelmed by a feeling of completeness when your baby is born and you hold her in your arms for the first time. A wonderful part of becoming a mum is the deep feeling of love you have for your baby, and the way that she gazes at you and snuggles into you for comfort. As your baby grows, you will often be the first person she wants when she's upset or uncertain, or just needing a cuddle. As a mother, you have a pivotal role within the family, providing love, care and nurture for both your baby and partner.

If you are at home with your baby, it's easy to feel you're 'just a mum', but your role is very important for the ongoing stability of your family. Having you as a constant and loving presence in life gives your baby confidence. I believe there is no higher calling in life than to be a mother, as you're bringing up a new generation and helping your child to be secure in his own worth and value. It's wonderful to watch your child developing new skills, and to be there to help and encourage him.

Most of us look back fondly on time spent with our mothers helping with practical things such as cooking or washing-up. It's a joy to spend time with your baby, helping her to feel part of what you're doing. You can also enrich your child's life with imaginary play, stories and creative activities like potato-printing or cutting and sticking. When you spend time with your baby in play or practical things, it helps her to know how special and precious she is to you.

The Challenges of Being a Mum

One of the major challenges of being a mother is a sense of loss of freedom and independence. Caring for your baby can seem all-consuming, particularly in the early days. You may feel very different from your friends who don't have children, and you may feel quite isolated at times. If you don't have close friends or family nearby, this can be particularly hard. Exhaustion and lack of sleep can also make it much more difficult for you to feel 'normal' enough to get out and see friends. Many of the mothers I've worked with have been surprised how much tiredness has affected them in all aspects of life.

It is very important as a mother to try to keep up some interests outside the home, so that you feel you have something for yourself. It's a good idea to regularly put aside half an hour or so for yourself, maybe to go to a gym or swimming pool that has a creche you can use. Some adult company is also important for your sanity as a new mother, so make time for seeing friends and family. Toddler and new baby groups (such as NCT groups) are also a great way of getting out and meeting new people with babies.

Within the first year of their baby's life, many mothers face the challenge of deciding whether to stay at home or return to work. In my experience, many first-time mothers feel quite keen to go back to work before their baby is born, but find in reality that it's a wrench to go back and they would much rather be at home. Try not to feel pressurized by either friends or work colleagues to make a decision before your baby is born. I always advise women to give themselves the first year at home with their baby, if at all possible. So much happens in this first year that you will never regret having had the time to be with your baby and watch him develop and grow.

Being a Working Mother

You may need or want to go back to work within the first year of your baby's life, and it's worth considering how to make this transition as smooth as possible for your whole family. If you are able to, give yourself some flexibility to see how the first month or so actually goes, and review how you're managing.

Try not to limit yourself to a time schedule of returning to work before your baby is born, and plan for more time off work than you think you might need. I always advise women to take at least the first six weeks off. You will need time to recover from delivery and sleep deprivation, and to establish your milk supply for breastfeeding. If you want to continue breastfeeding once you've returned to work, you will also need time to get used to expressing milk and organizing feeds.

Once you return to work, it's important not to get overloaded, as you can easily become exhausted with the demands of both work and caring for your baby. As far as possible, aim to be home early enough to spend time with your baby before she goes to bed. Before your baby is born, it's a good idea to consider whether you can work part-time or flexi-time to fit around family life. You may want to consider whether you and your partner could both work part-time. You may also be able to work from home; however, it's important to keep work demands within a set time of the day and consider what childcare support you will need.

Before you return to work, it's important to look at your options for childcare. Grandparents may be able to support you, or you may need to consider a childminder, day nursery or nanny. Before your baby's first day on his own in childcare, try to spend a few days helping him to settle in and feel safe with his carer. If your baby is going to a nursery, see if it's possible for the staff to give you a diary or update of what he has been doing that day. This can be a good way to feel in touch and involved with his day while you're working.

Being Parents and a Couple

In your new roles as parents, it's important to remember that neither of you can do it alone, and that you need one another. It will help your relationship if you praise each other's parenting and work collaboratively rather than competitively. As a mother, it's easy to become overprotective and feel that your partner isn't capable of looking after the baby as well as you can. However, it's important to give your partner space to learn parenting skills and spend time with the baby. Try not to criticize one another, and give each other the space to make a few mistakes along the way. If at all possible, try to share the practical aspects of baby care and support each other.

As well as being parents, you are still a couple, and you will find that you need some baby-free time together as your baby gets older. Your baby can easily take up all your attention and time; however, establishing a good routine will make it easier for you to put aside some time for your relationship. As your baby gets older and more independent, it gets easier to have time together as a couple. It's important to show physical affection to one another, even if you are not yet making love after your baby's birth. Once you resume lovemaking, don't forget that you need to consider contraception, and talk to your GP or family planning clinic about suitable contraception if you're breastfeeding.

It's amazing how much your baby will pick up on your behaviour as a couple. Even though your baby may not understand the words you are saying, she will be affected by raised voices or arguments. As much as you can, get into a habit of talking through difficult issues out of your baby's earshot. Set yourselves some ground rules, as these will continue to apply when your child is older and does understand what you are saying. Try to make time regularly to talk to each other about how you're feeling and how you're adjusting to becoming parents. You may also need to talk about how you're sharing the parental and domestic responsibilities, so that tension doesn't build up between you. Employing a cleaner or somebody to help with the ironing, even if just for a short period, can often help with these issues.

One of your baby's main needs in life is to know he's loved, and to know that you love each other as parents. A strong, loving relationship between the two of you helps your baby to grow up feeling secure. The love that you have for one another as a couple and as a family helps him to learn how to relate in a loving way to others around him. As your baby gets older, being united as parents regarding boundaries and discipline will strengthen your relationship and provide your baby with stability.

Becoming a Family

Relationship with Siblings

Brothers and sisters of twelve to eighteen months of age probably won't notice a new baby very much, as they are still babies themselves. The main focus for a child this age is having Mummy and Daddy's time and attention, so it's very important to give her lots of cuddles and include her as much as possible when a new baby comes home. Children of this age usually get used to having a new baby around so quickly that they will soon not remember a time without a baby brother or sister. As far as possible, keep your toddler's routine the same as before the baby was born, and spend as much one-to-one time with her as you can.

Many families ask me about preparing their toddler for the arrival of a new baby. I advise that you don't tell your toddler too soon about your pregnancy, as it can seem like a very long, boring wait for a young child. Once you have a visible bump and the baby is moving, your older child can feel your tummy and share in the excitement about a new brother or sister. You can show your toddler ultrasound scan pictures or books to help explain what's happening. Before you go into hospital, it's important that your older child knows that you will be away for a short time, and that you tell him who will be coming to look after him. If you are moving your toddler out of his cot or the nursery, make sure that you do this either a good couple of months before the baby is due or leave it until about three months afterwards so that he doesn't feel pushed out by the arrival of the new baby.

When your toddler first meets the baby, it can be a good idea to have a present for him from his new brother or sister. Be aware that your toddler may feel very jealous of the new baby, and may lash out or hit her when you are not watching. Don't leave your toddler and baby together unattended, and try to show your toddler how to gently care for the baby, praising him when he handles the baby gently. Some toddlers feel very excluded at feed times, so either settle him down for a nap (if it is nap time) while you feed, or encourage him to be with you and the baby, playing quietly or watching a video.

Brothers and sisters of about three years of age and over can feel very special if they have a role in caring for the baby, such as helping you to bath him or being the 'nappy monitor'. This will help your older child to feel part of the baby's life, and not excluded from the new relationship between you and the baby. As the baby starts moving about, try to have a separate area where older children can keep their own toys and play undisturbed by the baby. Older children's toys may be too fragile for babies, or small enough for them to put in their mouth and choke on. You can create separate play areas using stairgates or by opening out a playpen and securing it to the walls. As your children grow, it's a joy to see them playing and having fun together.

Grandparents can be an invaluable part of family life, providing support for both parents and grandchildren. Many grandparents are regularly involved in looking after grandchildren nowadays, often doing the school run or providing daytime childcare while parents are at work. It's important to make sure that grandparents are not overburdened, and that you have discussed whether any payment will be involved for childcare. Remember that grandparents' energy levels will not be the same as younger people's, and looking after grandchildren can be exhausting.

In the early days of your baby's life, it can be difficult to balance time with your baby on your own with involving grandparents so that they feel wanted and needed. However, if grandparents can get involved with practical things such as cooking meals or shopping for you, this can take pressure off you and help them to feel they have a role. As your baby gets older, grandparents will love having her to visit or stay, and this can help them to build a special relationship.

The Joys of Being a Grandparent

As a grandparent, don't worry that there's a formula you must fit into; you don't suddenly have to take up knitting if you've never fancied it before. Your own personality will have a unique impact on your grandchildren, and they will love you just as you are. It is a privilege to have an investment in your grandchildren's lives as they grow up.

One of the greatest joys of being a grandparent is spending time with your grandchildren. It's wonderful when your grandchildren first begin to recognize you and are excited to see you. It is a joy to know you're becoming a special part of their lives. If you live on your own, it can be particularly special to have your grandchildren around, as their company brings so much fun and energy. Visits from my own grandchildren have been tremendous fun, and it's wonderful to have quality time to spend with them and yet be able to hand them back at the end of the day.

As a grandparent, you often have the freedom to give your grandchildren lots of time, attention and affection. Grandfathers particularly may find that they can be more actively involved with their grandchildren than they were with their own children, and they can very much enjoy this special role. Outings and activities with you can enrich your grandchildren's lives, and will become treasured memories. It's wonderful to share in your grandchildren's achievements as they get older, and help them to know how proud you are of them. Being involved in your grandchildren's lives gives them a real sense of security and worth, knowing they're loved by you as well as their parents.

As your children adjust to being parents, you can provide a listening ear and help and encourage them in their parenting. I personally feel it is very important to let them know that they're doing a great job as parents, even if there are some areas where you feel you might do it differently. Try to avoid giving advice, and you will find it a joy when your children do ask you for help. Your children need affirmation, rather than advice or criticism. When you help out with your grandchildren, it's important to be as consistent as possible with the way your children are parenting. This will give your grandchildren stability, and help your children to feel they can trust you to back them up.

The Challenges of Being a Grandparent

One of the most challenging things as a grandparent is realizing that your children and their partners are a new family unit who need your respect. It can be tempting to give your own children advice, forgetting that they are now the parents, not you. As grandparents, you will have a different relationship with your own children than with your son- or daughter-in-law. Often, a son-in-law can feel very pushed out and resentful of his mother-in-law, particularly if she 'takes over' with the baby or outstays her welcome. Daughters-in-law often struggle with how to include both their own parents and in-laws, and as grandparents it's important to be able to stand back and not add to the pressure.

Grandparents are often surprised to find that there have been huge changes in approaches to bringing up children within a generation. I have talked to many friends with grandchildren, and they seem to have a number of similar observations and concerns about the way that their children cope with parenting. Many grandparents worry that young babies are carried around all the time and not put down to settle, meaning that parents lack time for themselves and become tired and overstretched. Grandparents often feel very concerned that parents are worn out by giving the grandchildren endless choices and entertainment. Grandparents also observe that grandchildren begin to exercise a 'right to rule', often leading to a chaotic household and frazzled parents. Many grandparents wish they could help their children to know that the grandchildren have a right to be loved, provided for, protected and affirmed, but not to control and demand.

It can be very difficult as a grandparent to stand back and avoid interfering in situations where you are concerned about how your grandchildren are being brought up, or how your children are coping. It's important not to criticize or give unwanted advice, as this can lead to a breakdown in the relationship with both your children and grandchildren. If you want to help, often the best thing you can do is be with your children, give them space to talk to you about how they're struggling and ask them how you could help.

As grandparents, it's important to recognize that your parenting may have been very different from your children's methods. If they do want you to help them with their parenting, you need to discuss this openly and find an approach you both agree on. It's a good idea to talk about what behaviour your children expect from the grandchildren, and how they'd like you to deal with unacceptable behaviour. If both you and your children are consistent, this will help the grandchildren to know where the boundaries are, and enable you to know that you're supporting rather than undermining your children's parenting.

Children can benefit greatly from time with their aunts, uncles and cousins. Some families have big get-togethers, and this can be a wonderful opportunity for children to get to know their wider family. My own grandchildren adore their Auntie Jayne and feel very special when they have time on their own with her. You may well find that your children find a young aunt or uncle much more fun to spend time with than you. If you don't have a large family, it can be great to have a circle of friends with children whom you see regularly and who can become an extended family for your child.

I hope this chapter will be a help to you as you settle into family life with your newborn. I cannot emphasize enough how important family members are to each other; try to remember that there is no such thing as the perfect family, and you don't get a practice run at parenting!

CHAPTER 13

The Spiritual and Emotional Needs of Your Child

If a child lives with criticism, he learns to condemn
If a child lives with hostility, he learns to fight
If a child lives with ridicule, he learns to be shy
If a child lives with shame, he learns to feel guilty

If a child lives with tolerance, he learns to be patient
If a child lives with encouragement, he learns confidence
If a child lives with praise, he learns to appreciate
If a child lives with fairness, he learns justice

If a child lives with security, he learns to have faith
If a child lives with approval, he learns to like himself
If a child lives with acceptance and friendship,
He learns to find love in the world.
    Dorothy Holt

Over the years as I've worked and travelled with clients and met many people, it has become increasingly clear that most people believe in some sort of spirituality. I personally believe that babies are not just body and mind, but have a spiritual side too. As parents, you instinctively care for your baby's physical needs, but you can also nurture his spiritual and emotional needs as he grows up.

I write as a Christian, so my thoughts come from that viewpoint; however, I hope that they will resonate with you whatever your own personal beliefs are. I believe in a loving God who made us with an inbuilt need to give and receive love. Even before your baby is born, a deep bond of love and connectedness will be growing between you and your child. I believe that God invented families, because he knows our needs, and longs for us to have the enjoyment, enrichment and fun of being together. In this chapter, I hope to help you explore your family's needs from a spiritual perspective.

I believe that the nature and character of God is love, and there are many aspects of this love that we can share as families. I believe that God can equip us as parents with love, joy, peace, patience, kindness and gentleness, faithfulness and self-control (Galatians 5:22–23).

Love

One of the special qualities of parental love is that parents love their children unconditionally. When we love a baby just for who she is, this gives her security, helps her to feel valued and enables her to trust people. As our children grow and we show them consistent love, we help them to know that they are treasured even when they are grumpy, miserable or upset. One of the ways that you can demonstrate love to your child is spending unhurried quality time with her in face-to-face contact and, as she grows, maybe looking at picture books, reading stories, or just playing games. This all helps to build up the confidence your child has in you and your love for her.

Joy

Babies and children are a great source of joy to us as parents, and our wider families. We all know the wonderful feeling when our baby smiles at us for the first time, and we know he recognizes us and is learning to respond. This feeling of joy goes on and on as he develops from stage to stage, with the fun of seeing him learning to roll over, sit up, crawl and then walk. There's huge pleasure in hearing him say his first word or helping him to learn to wave goodbye.

Children often have a wonderful natural sense of happiness, fun and freedom, which is very uplifting for parents. Amidst all the worries and tiredness of being a parent, times of joy, fun and exuberance are important. Enjoying each other's company and doing silly or fun things helps to bring you together as a family.

Peace

In the first few weeks of life, you will be amazed at the precious times of stillness and peace you have with your baby, particularly when feeding. Parents often feel overwhelmed with a sense of awe and wonder when they look at their baby at these quiet times. Take advantage of these early days to rest calmly with your baby, as this will bring a sense of peace to her too. As you bring up your children, talking and agreeing together on your approach to parenting helps you to be calm and peaceful as parents. This helps children to feel secure and safe.

Patience

Patience is a hugely important part of parenting; however, it is one of the first things that can slip when you're exhausted. When your baby is young, it can be difficult and frustrating when you are not sure how to meet his needs. However, persevering and being patient with both the baby and yourself will help him to feel safe and secure. As your child grows, it is often tempting to do things for him, rather than giving him the time to practise and make mistakes. However, you can give him tremendous confidence if you're patient with him as he learns new skills. In your relationship as parents, it is important to be as tolerant with one another as possible, as you are the role models for your child. Showing patience, rather than frustration, helps your child to learn to be patient with others.

Kindness and Gentleness

Babies and children blossom in a kind and gentle environment. Talking to your baby in a gentle, soft tone of voice helps her to know that she is safe and loved. Speaking words of encouragement and love to your child helps her to feel confident. Children pick up on unkind things we say about them, and we sometimes underestimate the effect this can have on their self-esteem. When we treat a child in a kind and gentle way, we help her to know that she's worthwhile, and not just a nuisance or in our way. In family life we can teach children how to show kindness to their siblings and other children as they grow up.

Faithfulness

We don't often use the word 'faithfulness' today, but it's important that children know that they have consistent, reliable parents who will love them faithfully. Just being there for our children and caring

178

for their needs daily assures them that they can trust us. We don't have to be super-parents, but being honest with our children about our own failings and being prepared to say sorry is all part of being faithful. It's important that we keep any promises we make to our children or each other. Being reliable and open with our children will help them not to be afraid of getting things wrong, and will encourage them to be honest and trusting with others.

Self-Control

'Train a child in the way he should go, and when he is old he will not turn from it.'
Proverbs 22:6

Learning self-control is a lifelong process, and it's our responsibility as parents to guide and direct our children. Through our own example, we can teach our children not to lash out when they are angry, or hurt others when they are upset. We can also help our children to understand that their wants will not always be met immediately, and that other people will sometimes come first. Giving our children clear boundaries helps them to know what is acceptable, and what behaviour we expect of them. As parents, it's important that we are self-controlled so that our own behaviour does not break these boundaries. In teaching and showing self-control within our families, we can help our children to live in harmony with others.

Faith in Family Life
Pregnancy and Birth

'For you created my inmost being, you knit me together in my mother's womb. I praise you because I am fearfully and wonderfully made.'
Psalm 139:13–14

I've noticed that the wonder of conception and pregnancy makes many parents think about the spiritual aspects of life. Bringing a new life into the world often makes us consider big questions such as 'Why am I here?' and 'Where is my life going?'

Long before he is born, many parents worry about the health and development of their baby. During my own pregnancies, I found great comfort in entrusting my children to God and praying for their safe delivery. I had a real sense of God being with me and caring for me as I went through labour and birth. Birth is an incredibly moving experience, and as parents we feel a huge sense of relief and achievement when we first hold our baby in our arms.

Welcoming Your Baby

You will probably feel incredibly thankful for the safe arrival of your baby, and many parents are stirred to offer a heartfelt prayer of thanks in the first hours of their baby's life. It can also be very special to celebrate your baby's life with friends and family at a later stage. You may want to give thanks for your baby in a formal ceremony such as a christening, or have an informal celebration at home. If you decide to have your baby christened, this can be an opportunity to look again at what you believe. I feel it's important to consider seriously whether you want to make promises to God if you're not sure whether you believe or not.

Prayer in Your Child's Life

> Dear Lord, I am so newly come
> I do not know my name.
> I do not even know yet Lord,
> If I am glad I came.
> Grant me the time to grow in love,
> Rejoice that I am here.
> Bless those who make me warm and dry.
> Lord, keep my mother near.
> *Dorothea Warren Fox*

As a Christian I believe that prayer is an important part of family life, and I prayed over my children from the very beginning of their lives. It was lovely to spend time praying for them in their cots at night, asking God to protect and care for them. As they grew up, praying for family and friends became part of their bedtime routine, and helped them to feel safe and secure.

Dealing with Hard Times

Nearly all of us at some stage go through difficulties that put pressure on family life. Illness, financial stress or relationship breakdown can lead us to wonder where God is and whether he is interested in us. Even when there have been no answers, I have personally found that having a deep faith in God and hanging onto his love has sustained me through times of real difficulty.

Enjoying Beauty in the World

As a mother of young children, I spent many happy hours with them as we went for walks together, exploring the wonder of nature and creation. We were very fortunate to bring our children up on a working farm, so that their involvement with the cows, sheep, ducks, hens, dogs and cats was all part of teaching them the value of life. Music was also a big part of our children's lives as they were growing up. I believe that such activities help to awaken children's spirituality, and are an important part of their development. Time spent taking part in these activities will draw you together as a family and give you some very special times that your children will never forget.

Conclusion

As we come to the end of this chapter, I hope that it will have given you more of an understanding of your family's spiritual needs from a Christian perspective. I hope also that it will have enabled you to think about how you are going to encourage and teach your children as they grow up, whatever your own personal beliefs are.

Quotations from Rachel's Clients

Lesley McCormack Gathy, September 2005

What really struck us was how easily Rachel helped our son fit into our family. What troubles me about other baby 'experts' who are out there is that they offer the one-baby, cookie-cutter approach. Rachel was able to come into our lives at a very special time – the arrival of our third and last baby. Her feeding and sleep schedules worked beautifully and I am convinced that the schedule she established for him during his first six weeks of life put him on course for the excellent eating and sleeping habits he (and we!) enjoy now that he's almost two. What Rachel instilled in us is that even in the same family you can and must vary your routines to fit into the schedule of the overall family. There are some basic principles you must apply but you need to provide yourself and the children with some flexibility in order for it to work properly for everyone. It's no good having the cookie-cutter approach to apply to every child and Rachel helped us establish a family formula that worked for us all and without anyone feeling overlooked or left out.

Ruth Gray, September 2005 (mother of twins)

I cannot stress how important having Rachel as a maternity nurse was. With one baby, no one had suggested a routine with me. With twins and an eighteen-month-old it was vital. Routine meant survival. Rachel helped me into a disciplined routine, and by the time she left after one month, they had dropped the night feed and were sleeping through the night. I am convinced that, because of the structure of Rachel's approach and consequently mine, they were, and still are, thriving, healthy, happy and relaxed boys. Life didn't end with three babies. Because I was helped to be organized, it was hard work but wonderful.

Kate Tew, September 2005

It's so hard to summarize what you did for all of us, but suffice to say you made what seemed at the time as the most challenging time of our lives straightforward, commonsensical, achievable, special, precious and normal. Your time with us all made us as parents realize, that although we had a very special baby, we could also help to have a very 'normal' child by being routine-orientated and providing a safe and secure family environment in which she could grow.

Although our daughter had been born with some unusual abnormalities and breastfeeding was not an option, you assured us that it was normal for babies to cry and that routine was key. You showed us how to be patient and let her settle herself and trust our own 'natural' instincts as parents as to when her crying was truly needy rather than anything else.

Julia Cuddihy Van Nice, September 2005

Rachel covers every topic from A to Z when it comes to caring for your baby – but also manages to make it all do-able. She is so keenly aware of a new mother's state of mind and utter exhaustion that she only focuses on what is truly important so that the mother can conserve her energy and not waste time worrying about insignificant details.

Julia Thomas-Everard, May 2005

The things we learnt from you were such a great help to us in our baby's first year... You taught us to use a rolled-up blanket along baby's back as you put him down on his side. This obviously made him feel really secure and he always slept well... You also taught us the importance of winding – no one ever explains the importance of this... You showed us how to do this properly and showed us... how to be patient waiting for the burp to come!

Maymie White, May 2005

Rachel was the first maternity nurse to teach me the value of letting a baby cry, and how that can be invaluable when setting up a routine.

My biggest fear with number one baby was failure. We are having babies later on in life, and are not used to failing at anything. Most of us have reached a fairly high position at work, are used to being in control and have a secret longing to carry that control through to motherhood – it's a shock.

Rachel's biggest achievement was ensuring the baby fitted in with our lives, and not the other way round. Dogs, husbands and other children need attention too!

Sally Turner, February 2005

Rachel's calm, gentle manner was just what my husband and I needed at a time when we both felt exhausted due to sleep deprivation and the shock of being parents for the first time. We have found that both our children have benefited from Rachel's excellent routine, which sets a good sleeping pattern from a very early age.

Marcia Middleton, May 2003

Rachel is, without doubt, a superb, highly experienced and gifted maternity nurse and comes exceptionally highly recommended by us. She has a wonderful, gentle affinity with babies, and seems to understand their every need. Equally, as a new mother I found her to be warm, kind, considerate and understanding to everything I was going through, and her knowledge and vast experience meant that she was able to offer invaluable advice and encouragement on every aspect of newborns and motherhood. Within hours of arriving at our home, each of my babies was calm and settled and she quickly established a wonderful routine which meant they were feeding well and sleeping through the night within a matter of weeks. As a mother this meant that I could enjoy and treasure every moment of this wonderful new experience without ever feeling overtired or anxious.

Mother from Somerset, May 2003

Rachel was kind, loving, gentle and patient with us all. She has a magic touch with babies, and clearly loves them. Rachel manages to impart information in an extremely gentle fashion, almost making one feel clever for having asked. This is exactly what one needs at such a time. She has vast experience of babies and children, and inspires great confidence.

Katherine Boscowen, March 2003

Rachel is highly professional and no child could start life in safer hands. She is calm, caring but firm, and understands a baby's needs instinctively. Not only is Rachel exceptional with babies but she provides a huge support for the mother and surrounding family.

Verity Edmiston, September 2001

Rachel is extremely well qualified in every aspect of childcare, bearing the characteristics of a traditional maternity nurse on the one hand and helping to keep the children and household in a calm and organized routine on the other. Rachel has proved her flexibility in any given situation and her endless experience and gentle manner make her truly a pleasure to have around.

Nick and Amanda Sullivan (whose three children Rachel worked with in 2004, 2000 and 1998)

Rachel is a calm and unflappable person who loves her work and the babies in her care. She is extremely competent and knows exactly what to do and she helped to build our own confidence in looking after our baby. She made the first few weeks very easy and enjoyable for us and prepared us for looking after him on our own.

Index

Further Resources

Useful addresses

Below are the addresses for some of the organisations mentioned in this book.

Association for Postnatal Illness

This organisation offers support to mothers suffering from postnatal illness.

145 Dawes Road,
Fulham,
London,
SW6 7EB,
Tel: 020 7386 0868
www.apni.org

Citizens Advice Bureau

The CAB has an informative website that will show you where your local advice bureau is.

www.adviceguide.org.uk

Cotton Bottoms

A UK delivery service that provides re-usable cotton nappies. They will collect them for washing and provide you with clean ones.

Cotton Bottoms Ltd
7-9 Water Lane Industrial Estate
Water Lane
Storrington
West Sussex
RH20 3XX
Tel : 08707 77 88 99
www.cottonbottoms.co.uk

Cry-sis

An organisation that provides help for parents with excessively crying, sleepless and demanding babies.

BM Cry-sis
London
WC1N 3XX
Cry-sis helpline 08451 228 669
www.cry-sis.org.uk

Lakeland Plastics

A company that specialises in useful kitchen gadgets.

Lakeland Limited
Alexandra Buildings
Windermere
Cumbria
LA23 1BQ
Tel: 015394 88100
www.lakelandlimited.co.uk

Useful books

These books give some good ideas on what to feed your baby.

Annabel Karmel, *New Complete Baby and Toddler Meal Planner*, 2004, Ebury Press
Nigella Lawson, *How to Eat: Pleasures and Principles of Good Food*, 1999, Chatto & Windus – see section on feeding babies